Praise
The Madrassa

"*This is a true benchmark study—it establis* Pakistan's vast educational/religious establi. recommendations on unprecedented fieldwork and judicious use of the existing literature. This will be an invaluable guide for policymakers, both in Pakistan and in the community of states that wish to help that state develop a truly modern and effective educational system.*"

—**Steven Cohen**, Brookings Institution

"*This study provides a comprehensive and objective assessment of Islamic education in Pakistan. Weighing the madrassah system's contribution to sectarianism, violent worldviews, and militancy, Fair methodically dispels many common myths about the country's religious schools. She also offers sound advice to U.S. policymakers anxious to encourage reforms.*"

—**Marvin Weinbaum**, Middle East Institute

"*This book provides a highly nuanced understanding of Pakistan society, the challenges and constraints the public education system in Pakistan faces, and the overall place and influence of religious schools in the country. The author is cognizant of the inflated attention that madaris have received from the international security community, especially in the past five years. This solidly researched work, strengthened further by field research, is an objective, welcome contribution which should help separate the fiction surrounding madaris from the reality.*"

—**Anita M. Weiss**, University of Oregon

The Madrassah Challenge
Militancy and Religious Education in Pakistan

The Madrassah Challenge

Militancy and Religious Education in Pakistan

C. Christine Fair

UNITED STATES INSTITUTE OF PEACE PRESS
Washington, DC

Cover: photos by C. Christine Fair

UNITED STATES INSTITUTE OF PEACE
1200 17th Street NW, Suite 200
Washington, DC 20036-3011
www.usip.org

First published 2008

Printed in the United States of America

The paper used in this publication meets the minimum requirements of American National Standards for Information Science—Permanence of Paper for Printed Library Materials, ANSI Z39.48-1984.

Library of Congress Cataloging-in-Publication Data

Fair, C. Christine.
The Madrassah Challenge: Militancy and Religious Education in Pakistan / C. Christine Fair.—1st ed.
    p. cm.
  Includes bibliographical references and index.
  ISBN 978-1-60127-028-3 (pbk. : alk. paper)
1. Madrassah—Pakistan. 2. Islamic religious education—Pakistan. 3. Religious militants—Pakistan. 4. Islamic fundamentalism—Pakistan. 5. Education and state—Pakistan. I. Title.
  BP43.P18F35 2007
  297.7'7095491—dc22
                                                        2007041262

To my beloved husband, Jeffrey D. Kelley,
who has tolerated long stays from home and long hours.
He is everything to me.

Contents

Foreword

Since the founding of the first madrassah in eleventh-century Baghdad, madaris (the plural of madrassah) have been bastions of Islamic religious orthodoxy. Their core curriculum has remained unchanged. Over the centuries, millions of theologians and religious judges (*muftis* and *qadis*) have been trained at madaris in knowledge of the Quran, Hadith, and Islamic jurisprudence. In one sense, the madaris were comparable to orthodox religious seminaries in other religious traditions. But the rise to power of the Taliban in Afghanistan changed the perception of the West about madaris. As the Taliban emerged from Pakistani seminaries to impose their brand of radical, antimodern, and brutal Islamic rule in Afghanistan, the image of a madrassah as the training center for young Islamist zealots took root.

Before the terrorist attacks of September 11, 2001, U.S. and European policymakers were more interested in the thoughts of Western-educated Muslims responsible for energy policy in Arab countries than those of half-literate mullahs trained at obscure seminaries. But Taliban leaders, who had ruled Afghanistan since the mid-1990s in the aftermath of Afghanistan's brutal civil war, were the products of madaris in Pakistan, and their role as protectors of al Qaeda terrorists has generated keen interest in their alma maters. Several journalists visiting the Darul Uloom Haqqania (Center of Righteous Knowledge), situated on the main highway between Islamabad and Peshawar, in the small town of Akora Khattak, spoke of the conservative school as "the University of Jihad."

The transformation and global spread of madaris during the 1980s and 1990s owes much to geopolitics, sectarian struggles, and technology, but the schools' influence and staying power derive from deep-rooted socioeconomic conditions that have so far proved resistant to change. Now, with the prospect of madaris churning out tens of thousands of would-be militant graduates each year, calls for reform are growing. But change in the schools' curriculum, approach, or mind-set is unlikely to be easy.

In some ways, madaris are at the center of a civil war of ideas in the Islamic world. Westernized and usually affluent Muslims lack an interest

in religious matters, but religious scholars, marginalized by modernization, seek to assert their own relevance by insisting on orthodoxy. A
regular education costs money and is often inaccessible to the poor, but
madaris are generally free. Poor students attending madaris find it easy
to believe that the West, loyal to uncaring and aloof leaders, is responsible for their misery and that Islam as practiced in its earliest form can
deliver them.

Madaris have been around since the Seljuk Vizier Nizam ul-Mulk
Hassan bin Ali Tusi founded a seminary in Baghdad to train experts in
Islamic law in the eleventh-century. Islam had become the religion of a
large community, stretching from North Africa to Central Asia. But
apart from the Quran, which Muslims believe to be the word of God
revealed through the Prophet Mohammad, and scattered records of
Hadith, the sayings of Prophet Mohammad, no definitive theological
texts existed.

The dominant Muslim sect, the Sunnis, did not have a clerical class,
leaving groups of believers to follow whoever inspired them in religious
matters. But Sunni Muslim rulers legitimated their rule through religion, depending primarily on an injunction in the Koran binding believers to obey the righteous ruler. Over time, it became important to seek
religious conformity and to define dogma to ensure obedience of subjects and to protect rulers from rebellion. Nizam ul-Mulk's madrassah
was intended to create a class of *ulema* (theologians), *muftis* (jurist-con-
sults), and *qadis* (judges) who would administer the Muslim empire,
legitimize its rulers as righteous, and define an unalterable version of
Islam.

Largely unchanged and unchallenged, this approach to education
dominated the Islamic world for centuries, until the advent of colonial
rule, when Western education penetrated countries previously ruled by
Muslims. Throughout the Middle East, as well as in British India and
Dutch-ruled Indonesia, modernization marginalized madaris. Their
graduates were no longer employable as judges or administrators as the
Islamic legal system gave way to Western jurisprudence. Muslim societies became polarized between madrassah-educated mullahs and the
economically prosperous, Western-educated individuals attending
modern schools and colleges.

But the poor remained faithful. The failings of the postcolonial elite in most Muslim countries paved the way for Islamic political movements such as al-Ikhwan al-Muslimin (the Muslim Brotherhood) in the Arab world, Jamaat-e-Islami (the Islamic Party) in South Asia, and the Nahdatul Ulema (the Movement for Religious Scholars) in Indonesia. These movements questioned the legitimacy of the Westernized elite, created reminders of Islam's past glory, and played on hopes for an Islamic utopia. In most cases, the founders of Islamic political movements were religiously inclined politicians with a modern education; madaris provided the rank and file.

The Iranian Revolution and the Soviet occupation of Afghanistan, both in 1979, inspired a profound shift in the Muslim world—and in the madaris. Iran's mullahs had managed to overthrow the shah and take power, undermining the idea that religious education was useless in worldly matters. Although Iranians belong to the minority Shiite sect of Islam, and their madaris have always had a more political character than Sunni seminaries, the image of men in turbans and robes running a country provided a powerful demonstration effect and politicized madaris everywhere.

Ayatollah Khomeini's revolutionary regime promised to export its revolutionary Shiite ideas to other Muslim states. Saudi Arabia and other Gulf countries began to pour money into Sunni madaris that rejected the Shiite theology of Iran, fund ulema who declared the Shiite Iranian model unacceptable to Sunnis, and call for a fight against Western decadence rather than Muslim rulers.

In the midst of this conflict, and the madrassah boom it spawned, the United States helped create an Islamic resistance to communism in Afghanistan, encouraging Saudi Arabia and other oil-rich states to fund the Afghan resistance and its supporters throughout the Muslim world. Pakistan's military ruler at the time, General Mohammed Zia ul-Haq, decided to establish madaris instead of modern schools in Afghan refugee camps, where five million displaced Afghans provided a natural supply of recruits for the resistance. The refugees needed schools; the resistance needed mujahideen. Madaris would provide an education of sorts, but it was believed that they would also serve as a center of indoctrination and motivation.

Pakistan was affected profoundly by the madrassah boom. It had 244 madaris in 1956. In recent years, the number has risen to several thousand. Pakistan's budgetary allocation for public education is inadequate for its burgeoning population, leaving large segments of the poor population without schooling. Madaris fill the education gap, especially for the poor. In the process, the number of madaris with ties to Islamist radicals has also increased, though it still reflects a minuscule proportion of total Pakistani madaris. While not all Islamist radicals come from madaris, Pakistani authorities have often described the madaris as being the central source for the rise of radical Islamism and terrorism.

The nature and extent of the security and social challenge posed by the madaris has seldom been methodically studied by American scholars. Much of the information about madaris in the United States, especially from Pakistan, is anecdotal. In *The Madrassah Challenge*, Christine Fair fulfills the need for an empirical study of the structure, pervasiveness, and nature of Pakistan's madaris.

This study reflects data on madrassah enrollment as well as assessing the quality and impact of a madrassah education. It goes beyond the rhetorical statements in the usual media coverage about "the dominant role" of madaris in Islamist radical movements and paints an honest picture of the madrassah within the context of the overall educational situation of Pakistan. Instead of arousing fear, *The Madrassah Challenge* helps in understanding the relationship between militancy and religious education in Pakistan and analyzes the various ideas for madrassah reform.

Husain Haqqani

Acknowledgments

I am grateful to Sayed Rashid Bukhari, who conducted fieldwork with me in February 2006. His insights and access to the madrassah world were the most important contributions to this effort. I am also indebted to the Pakistani officials and analysts, as well as the numerous madrassah administrators, teachers, and students, who were generous with their hospitality and frank in sharing their views, despite their numerous concerns about the intentions of this American female researcher with decidedly bad taste in *shalwar kameez*.

Special thanks are owed to Vali Nasr of the Naval Postgraduate School and Mahin Karim of the National Bureau of Asian Research (NBAR), who provided painstaking and critical reviews of earlier drafts of this monograph. NBAR funded fieldwork for this study.

I am grateful to Dietrich Reetz (Zentrum Moderner Orient, Berlin) and Claudia Preckel (Ruhr-Universität Bochum, Bochum), who chaired a panel at the 2006 meeting of the European Association for South Asian Studies in Leiden, where I presented this work in July 2006. Reetz, Preckel, and the participants in that panel shared their vast and numerous insights, which were incorporated into this text. Thanks also to Qamar-ul Huda and Pamela Aall of the United States Institute of Peace, who provided internal reviews of the manuscript. Pavi Banavar provided helpful edits of various versions of this manuscript and deserves many thanks for her patience and hard work. I am also indebted to Anita Weiss and an anonymous external reviewer; both gave extensive constructive feedback. Finally, I owe a special debt to Linda Rabben for providing excellent editorial guidance. Any and all errors that persist, despite the best efforts of numerous colleagues who provided feedback, are the responsibility of the author alone.

Glossary

Aaliyah: Two-year program of religious studies that follows Thanviyah, e-Khassah (see below).

Alim (pl. *ulama*): Scholar of Islamic religion and law.

Alimiyah: Two-year program of religious studies that follows Aaliyah.

al-uloom al-aqliya: Rational sciences, such as philosophy, geometry, medicine, chemistry, and geography. Often contrasted to *al-uloom al-naqliya* (religiously "transmitted" sciences).

al-uloom al-naqliya: "Transmitted sciences," such as reading and interpreting Quran and Hadith (traditions and sayings of the Prophet Muhammad). Sometimes called traditional or religious sciences. Often understood in contrast to al-uloom al-aqliya.

Ahl-e-Hadith: Sunni interpretative tradition associated with Hanbali school of jurisprudence (in Pakistan sometimes called Salafist).

Barelvi: Usually refers to the followers of Imam Ahmed Raza Khan Barelvi, an important Muslim scholar of the late nineteenth and early twentieth centuries. Barelvis tend to observe practices that are Sufi in orientation, such as worship at the graves of religious leaders and the acceptance of rituals associated with this religious tradition.

Dars-e-Quran: Literally, study of the Quran. Informal study sessions that convene at a home or a mosque.

Dars-i-Nizami: Curriculum devised by Mullah Nizamuddin Sihalvi (d.1748), a scholar in Islamic jurisprudence and philosophy based at Farangi Mahal (a famous madrassah in Lucknow).[1] Not the same curriculum propounded by Mullah Nasiruddin Tusi (d.1064) at the Nizamia madrassah he established in eleventh-century Baghdad. Almost all Sunni madaris—irrespective of whether their sectarian affiliation is Barelvi, Ahl-e-Hadith, Jamaat-i-Islami, or Deobandi—follow this course of study, formally adopted by the Deoband seminary in 1867. Shia madaris have a similar multiyear curriculum. (See *Deobandi.*)

darul uloom: Universities.

daura: Literally, a tour. Here, a tour of religious proselytization, often in the service of specific groups, such as Tablighi Jamaat.

dawa: Literally, "summons" or "invitation." Implies proselytizing to non-Muslims to embrace Islam and to Muslims to become better Muslims, variously defined. (See *Tablighi Jamaat.*)

Deobandi: School of Islam that emerged from a Muslim religious revival movement in the South Asian subcontinent during British rule. Began in the town of Deoband in modern-day India. Originated as a puritanical movement to uplift Muslims by purifying Islamic practices through, among other things, discouraging mystical beliefs, such as intercession by saints and propitiation at graves and shrines.

fauqani: Madrassah education. Generally takes eight years in four two-year stages, beginning with Thanviyah-e-Ammah and ending with Alimiyah.

fiqh: Islamic jurisprudence.

Hadith: The sayings, actions, and thoughts of the Prophet Muhammad. With the Quran it comprises the sunna (Islamic law). Scholars of various interpretative traditions disagree about the legitimacy of various Hadith texts in the interpretative traditions within Islam.

hafez: One who has memorized the Quran.

Hanafi: Dominant school of Islamic jurisprudence in Pakistan and South Asia generally. Considered to be the most liberal of the four schools of *fiqh* (jurisprudence) because it accepts both analogical reasoning and unanimity in decision making.

Hanbali: One of the four schools of fiqh within Sunni Islam. The most rigid of the four schools, as it rejects both analogical reasoning and unanimity in decision making. The foundation of Wahhabi thought.

Hifz-e-Quran: Memorizing the Quran.

Ibtedai: Literally, "primary." The first level (five years) of religious education, roughly equivalent to the period of primary education in the worldly sector.

Islamiyat: Islamic studies. An official component of Pakistan's state curriculum.

Jamaat-i-Islami: Supra-sectarian Islamist political party in Pakistan.

jamia: Colleges

madrassah (pl. *madaris):* School that imparts secondary and postsecondary religious education using a specialized curriculum, Dars-i-Nizami.

maktab (pl. *makatib):* Religious primary school that generally teaches young children to read the Quran and sometimes to recite it.

markaz: Literally, "center." Headquarters or central offices of an organization. In the context of this study, the central locations of the five boards that govern Pakistan's madaris.

maslak (pl. *masalik):* Way or practice, usually in reference to a particular interpretive tradition.

matriculation ("matric"): Certificate on completion of ten years of education and passage of an examination. Matric qualification is a prerequisite for many jobs in Pakistan as well as admission to colleges and universities.

maulvi: Religious scholar.

Mutawassitah: First level of formal religious education that follows Ibtedai. Three years long, it is the equivalent of middle school. (See *Vustani.*)

Nazira-e-Quran: Learning to properly recite the Quran.

nisab: Curriculum.

qari (alt. *qazi):* One who has mastered the recitation of the Quran in one of the seven major styles of recitation, *tajweed.*

radd: Refutation.

Tablighi Jamaat: Deobandi-influenced organization dedicated to the propagation of authentic Islam (dawa). Aims to cleanse Islam of *shirk*, beliefs and practices inconsistent with orthodox Islam and rooted in local, pre-Islamic beliefs.

tafseer: Exegesis of the Quran.

Takmeel: Typically a one-year, post-M.A. course of religious study.

Thanviyah-e-Ammah: Two-year level of religious studies that follows Mutawassitah.

Thanviyah-e-Khassah: Two-year level of religious studies that follows Thanviyah-e-Ammah.

ulama: See **Alim**.

umma: The global Muslim community, the community of Islamic faithful.

Vustani: First level of formal religious education that follows Ibtedai. Three years long, the equivalent of middle school. (See **Mutawassitah**.)

wafaq: School of thought (maslak). Usually translated as "board"—as in school board. There are five such boards (four Sunni and one Shia), and most of Pakistan's madaris are affiliated with one of them.

zakat: Almsgiving. Muslims donate a percentage of their annual earnings as alms or charity. The amount differs according to Sunni and Shia traditions.

Acronyms

B.A.	Baccalaureate
ESR	Education Sector Reform
F.A.	Fine Arts
FATA	Federally Administered Tribal Agencies
IIU	International Islamic University
IRIT	Iqra Rozatul Itfal Trust
ITMD	Ittehad-e-Tanzimat Madaris-e-Diniya
JI	Jamia Tafeem ul Quran
JUI	Jamiat-ul-Ulama-i-Islam
JUI-F	JUI-Fazlur Rehman
M.A.	Master of Arts
MMA	Muttahida Majlis-e-Amal
MRA	Ministry of Religious Affairs
NWFP	Northwest Frontier Province
PEIP	Private Educational Institutions of Pakistan
PEMBO	Pakistan Education Madaris Board Ordinance
PIHS	Pakistani Integrated Household Survey
PME	Pakistan Madrassah Education Ordinance
PML-Q	Pakistan Muslim League-Qaid
SPDC	Social Policy and Development Center
SRA 1860	Societies Registration Act of 1860
SSP	Sipah-e-Sahaba-e-Pakistan
UNICEF	United Nations Children's Education Fund
USAID	United States Agency for International Development
WAPDA	Water and Power Development Authority

Introduction

Pakistan's madaris (plural of madrassah or seminary) have attracted the attention of policymakers in the United States and elsewhere since the 9/11 terrorist attacks. Even though none of the attackers studied in madaris in Pakistan or elsewhere, madaris are alleged to be incubators of militants in Pakistan and responsible for creating communities of support for militancy in the region. Consequently the United States, the United Kingdom, and other nations have strongly encouraged Pakistan's President Pervez Musharraf to reform these institutions and close down madaris that may have links to militant groups. An ever-expanding body of literature continues to concentrate upon the importance that Pakistan's madaris supposedly have to the security of South Asia and beyond.[1]

Despite this proliferation of analysis and the security threats allegedly posed by madaris, numerous fundamental questions persist regarding the number of madaris in Pakistan, their share of the educational market, the socioeconomic background of madrassah students, the connections between madaris and militancy, Islamabad's sincerity in reforming the madrassah system, and the support among madrassah leadership, educators, and students for such reform.

This study aims to address these questions in considerable detail, synthesizing several different kinds of data, including information obtained from interviews with madrassah officials, teachers, and students in Pakistan; discussions with U.S., British, French, and Pakistani governmental and nongovernmental analysts; and numerous survey data and opinion polls.[2] It draws on secondary literature, recent scholarship on terrorist recruitment preferences and terrorist labor supply, and analyses of educational economics and school choice in Pakistan. I have also used the longstanding literature on Islamic educational institutions in Pakistan.

The first chapter situates religious education in Pakistan in the larger context of the country's educational system. The premise is that a complex appreciation of religious education in Pakistan requires a more comprehensive understanding of how education takes place generally and the various venues besides madaris in which religious education takes place. This chapter describes and, where appropriate and possible, enumerates the different kinds of schools in Pakistan and identifies where religious education is available in the schools. It also provides data on educational enrollment and attainment in Pakistan's various educational sectors, including variations across time, geography, and student socioeconomic background. I present available information on educational funding generally, and religious education in particular, and conclude with a discussion of family preferences with respect to education and the ways in which the educational market is innovating to keep pace with these evolving preferences.

The second chapter covers the variety and organization of both formal and informal religious educational institutions, with particular focus on the formal institutions (the madaris). It presents available information about madrassah faculty and students and their activities. For instance, it has been alleged that madaris constitute "vote banks" and "street power" for Islamist parties. In this chapter I try to address the veracity of these and other claims and counterclaims made by madrassah officials and educators.

The third chapter presents empirically grounded arguments that cast doubt about unqualified and sweeping claims that madaris writ large produce militants in Pakistan. Instead, this monograph argues that madaris are less relevant for recruiting militants for the Kashmir and Indian theaters, where better qualified recruits seem to be preferred. However, some madaris in the border areas and in the Pakistani hinterland may have a limited role in transnational terrorism and may play a critical role in the insurgency in Afghanistan, especially with respect to suicide attackers operating there. A few madaris also appear to be important for the recruitment of suicide attackers within Pakistan, and there is evidence that some madaris are implicated in sectarian violence inside Pakistan.

The scale of sectarian violence in Pakistan is staggering, with hundreds of people killed or injured in such attacks each year. In 2006 alone, the New Delhi–based Institute for Conflict Management recorded thirty-six sectarian attacks in Pakistan that claimed the lives of 201 persons and injured another 349.[3] The Islamabad-based Pak Institute for

Peace Studies puts the number of sectarian attacks at forty-one.[4] This chapter also presents limited evidence linking madaris and *support* for militancy (jihad)—even if madaris have only limited involvement in the recruitment of militants writ large. That is, madaris may help create an atmosphere conducive to jihad in the region, even though madrassah students are not well represented across the ranks of all militant organizations.

In the fourth chapter I discuss Islamabad's efforts to reform madaris. Drawing extensively from fieldwork, I present a complex set of reform-related issues from the viewpoints of the government, the madaris' administrators and educators, and Islamic scholars.

The final chapter lays out the most important conclusions and policy implications and suggests a number of policy initiatives that might address some of the fundamental concerns emanating from ostensible ties between education and security inside and outside Pakistan. Analyses of nationally representative household surveys find that the public school sector educates about 70 percent of Pakistan's full-time enrolled students. Because the problems within Pakistan's public educational sector also present daunting challenges with clear security implications, this study offers a number of policy options that cover the entire educational market—not just the religious educational sector.

The Literature on Pakistan's Madaris: A Critical Appraisal

Before 2001 few American policymakers had heard of Pakistan's religious schools or madaris. Because madrassah means "school," some writers and analysts use the adjective *deeni* (religious) to make it clear that they mean religious schools rather than schools generally. Jessica Stern's writings have advanced the belief that Pakistan's madaris are factories of ideological indoctrination and even military training for terrorist organizations throughout Pakistan and South Asia.[5] Following the September 11 terrorist attacks on the United States and the accompanying scrutiny of Pakistan, the attention of state and international nonstate entities alike increasingly focused on these educational institutions. The popular press was rife with varying estimates of the numbers of madaris in

Pakistan, the numbers of students enrolled in such schools, and their purported links to terrorism. Apart from press reports, a number of scholars, research institutions, and advocacy organizations advanced the notion that Pakistan's madaris posed a serious threat, not only to the stability of the South Asian region but also to U.S. national security interests. Stern's writings were crucial in encouraging this fixation upon madaris. Other scholars, including Peter Singer and Robert Looney, also took up the issue, albeit with greater skepticism about both the links between madaris and militancy and the prevailing estimates of the number of madaris.[6]

The International Crisis Group (ICG) issued a report in 2002 that advanced debate on the dangers posed by madaris. It claimed that about a third of all students in Pakistan were enrolled in them.[7] Perhaps more than any other, this finding brought the weight of the international community down upon these institutions. The import of this report is reflected by the fact that the director of ICG in Pakistan, Samina Ahmed, was asked to testify before the Senate Foreign Affairs Committee in April 2005 about the connections between madaris and terrorism.[8]

The timing of the report was important for at least two reasons. First, its publication followed the September 11 terrorist attacks in the United States and resulting concern about Pakistan as a frontline state in the war on terrorism in light of the country's problematic history with terrorist groups and the Taliban. Second, it was released during the 2001–02 military confrontation between India and Pakistan. This standoff was precipitated by a terrorist attack on the Indian parliament, allegedly executed by Jaish-e-Muhammad, a Pakistan-based militant organization associated with al Qaeda. This attack demonstrated that Pakistan-based groups were a menace domestically, as well as to regional and even global security interests.

Since 2005 several scholarly articles and editorials have sought to contribute an alternative view of madaris. In the *New York Times Book Review* in December 2005, William Dalrymple summarized the conclusions of several scholars who argued that the links between madaris and militancy had been greatly exaggerated. Nonetheless, he contended that madaris constitute an "education system running parallel to the moribund state sector," and few "make any effort to prepare their students to function in a modern, plural society."[9] It is difficult to understand how a system that claims perhaps less than 1 percent of the full-time educational market share can meaningfully be termed a parallel educational system.[10]

Peter Bergen and Swati Pandey examined the backgrounds of seventy-nine terrorists involved in five of the worst anti-Western terrorist attacks (the 1993 World Trade Center bombing, the 1998 bombings of two U.S. embassies in Africa, the September 11, 2001, attacks, the 2002 Bali nightclub bombing, and the London bombings in July 2005). They found madrassah involvement to be rare and further noted that the masterminds of the attacks all had university degrees.[11] Bergen and Pandey's findings are consistent with earlier conclusions by Marc Sageman and others who have studied terrorist characteristics and concluded that madaris are less correlated than institutions of higher learning with production of terrorists.[12] Alexander Evans also wrote a lucid analysis of the varied roles of madaris in the Muslim world and presented compelling evidence against the popular notion that they constitute threats to regional and international security.[13]

Why do analyses of security and madaris present such contradictory findings? Part of the problem is that with few exceptions, scholars have tended to rely predominantly on one kind of data or one analytical lens to interpret these data. Most of the current works on the subject (nearly every popular press account, Stern, Singer, the ICG) have relied almost exclusively on interview data from inside or outside Pakistan.[14] Few of these studies have utilized the well-developed literature on madaris in Pakistan and South Asia, including the works of Mumtaz Ahmad, Jamil Malik (one of the first scholars of madaris), Muhammad Qasim Zaman, J.K. Kran, Barbara Metcalf, and Francis Robinson, among others.[15]

Regrettably these research efforts fail to utilize various quantitative studies to corroborate their interview data. This is unfortunate because quantitative data for Pakistan's madaris are numerous and include surveys conducted by Saleem Mansoor Khalid of the Institute of Policy Studies, Tariq Rahman, several surveys of madaris in Pakistan carried out by the government of Pakistan in 1979, 1988, 2000, and data from national household surveys (such as the Pakistani Census and the Pakistani Integrated Household Survey, or PIHS) that collect information on household school utilization.[16]

The work of Saleem Ali is commendable because it seeks to combine interview data with other forms of survey data (some collected by Ali's research team).[17] Using incident data in two districts (Ahmedpur and Islamabad), Ali found that sectarian violence correlated strongly and positively with madrassah penetration. The primary weakness of his study is that it does not reflect significant knowledge of the operations of militant groups in Pakistan. The data he collected and analyzed contain inherent sample biases that limit the generalizability of the results.[18] Nonetheless, Ali's work makes great strides in incorporating different kinds of data with which to analyze the apparent madrassah problem.

Data Caveats

Tahir Andrabi's study (commissioned by the World Bank) and the Islamabad-based Social Policy and Development Center (SPDC) provide solid evidence about the penetration of madaris in the educational market for full-time enrollments and the variations of madrassah market share across much of Pakistan and over time. Using household data from the 1998 census and the Pakistani Integrated Household Survey, both the Andrabi team and the SPDC determined that full-time madrassah enrollments may be less than 1 percent nationwide.[19] Although the Andrabi and SPDC efforts—as well as those of other quantitative analysts—yield numerous insights about the determinants of family choice with respect to religious, public, and private schooling options, they do little to illuminate the lingering policy questions about the connections between madaris and militancy. Nor do these studies of school choice adequately acknowledge that religious education is not confined to the madrassah and other religious educational institutions. Thus, although the majority of full-time enrolled students may study in public schools, this does not mean that they are not studying religious subjects.

Because the quantitative findings of Andrabi and SPDC are used extensively in this study, it is worthwhile to note their limitations as well as their strengths. First, they rely on household-based surveys, which may exclude some potential madrassah students (such as orphans or homeless children) and are somewhat dated (The most recent data are from 2001). Recognizing that household surveys underestimate madrassah utilization, the Andrabi team adjusted their estimates to account for excluded groups and population growth. Their adjusted figures suggest generously that 475,000 children—less than 3 percent of all full-time enrollments—might attend madaris *full time*.[20]

Another limitation of the studies using household surveys is that these data do not include the Federally Administered Tribal Agencies (FATA) and protected areas of the Northwest Frontier Province, where madrassah enrollment could be much higher.[21] The Andrabi team presents evidence that this may be the case: Intensity of madrassah enrollment was highest along the Pakistan-Afghanistan border, reaching 7.5 percent in the district of Pishin. This raises the possibility that intensity of madrassah utilization could be just as high, if not higher, in all or part of FATA. For these reasons estimates of madrassah utilization could be underestimated, particularly in areas such as FATA and restricted areas of NWFP. The Andrabi team could not correct estimates to account for this exclusion because of the scant empirical bases for such correction.[22] The lack of visibility in this critical area is deeply problematic. Pakistan's madaris in FATA—especially in North and South Waziristan—are deeply implicated in the recruitment of suicide attackers in both Afghanistan and Pakistan.[23]

Finally, the 1998 census itself is the subject of much controversy, apart from the sampling issues noted above. Despite a long history of census taking—dating to the census system introduced by the British in the mid-nineteenth century—successive governments delayed the 1990 census until 1998. The government cited security-related reasons for the delay. In fact, its motivations were related more to domestic political concerns. The government resisted enumerating the population because numerous demographic changes (population growth, age structure, literacy, ethnic composition, and so forth) were anticipated. These could have important implications for the allocation of government representation, resources, and social privileges and would encourage the political mobilization of minorities whose numbers had increased.[24]

The state also feared that a population growth rate above 3 percent would draw adverse attention from the international community and indicate inadequate efforts to invest in Pakistan's women.[25] In addition, millions of ethnic Pashtun refugees from Afghanistan were still in Pakistan. At least partly because of longstanding concerns about Pashtun nationalism and even separatism, the government had hoped that some of the Afghan refugees would have been repatriated before the election. Because of the various controversies surrounding the conduct of the 1998 census, its data have attracted numerous critics. For that reason this study does not rely exclusively on findings from the 1998 census. However, as will be shown, findings from the census are similar to those obtained using other data sources.[26]

Because of these data limitations and because of the tendency in some disciplines to devalue survey data, scholars such as the Andrabi team who have relied upon these data have been criticized. While the caveats noted above are necessary to note, it is also important to underscore the value of these data and to address some of the criticisms made about their use. Whereas SPDC has used their data without generating controversy, the work of Andrabi came under fire even though his results with the PIHS were identical to those of the SPDC. These critiques problably were fueled by those ideologically commited to the notion that madaris are vehicles for mass instruction. The Andrabi team also pointed out a critical arithmetic error of the ICG report, which immediately subjected their report to widespread criticism that often was not scholarly in nature or tone.

However, these survey data and the Andrabi study are valuable for numerous reasons. First, notwithstanding the various limitations of the PIHS and the census data, analyses of these data yield comparable results despite their different sampling methodologies and questionnaire designs. Those results suggest that the data allow analysts to agree on a stable, and thus defensible, result regarding full-time madrassah utilization. Second, and related to the first reason, both the PIHS and census instruments are clear about the data elements they collect: household utilization of different educational institutions for children studying fulltime. Thus one can speak clearly about full-time enrollments in madaris and other schools. Most interview data do not make any effort to disaggregate intensity of utilization, partly because it is impossible to do so by relying upon interlocutors' accounts.

Third, the Andrabi team embraces the various sample biases and other limitations of the data and seeks to use sophisticated corrective measures to account for them. One of the means by which they sought to address the various sample biases included sampling all households within several villages of districts in the Punjab. This was necessary because in the household surveys madrassah utilization was a rare event. To understand how madrassah utilization differs across households, one needs a solid sample size of households that use madaris for at least one child.

Several commentators criticized the reliance on Punjab-derived data to correct for undercounting in the household surveys and to determine differences between and among households in their schooling choices. Such critics wrongly claim that the Punjab is unusually low in madrassah utilization and therefore unsuitable for such analyses. Unfortunately these arguments are empirically impoverished. The Punjab has the largest concentration of madaris in Pakistan, at least partly because it is the country's most populous province, as shown later in this monograph. Thus madrassah utilization in Punjab accounts for a large proportion of Pakistani madrassah customers; indeed, it is entirely defensible to use these data to cast light on undercounting of madrassah students in household surveys and on inter- and intra-household variation in school choice.

The tendency of scholars of the madrassah policy problem to apply one kind of data and one analytical lens no doubt results from academic specialization. But the variegated findings in the various treatments of madaris and their concomitant policy implications underscore the fact that a holistic understanding of Islamic education in Pakistan and its security implications demands a multidisciplinary analytical approach that integrates several kinds of data. For these reasons, to the greatest extent possible this monograph incorporates and synthesizes different kinds of data and different interpretative frameworks to illuminate whether madaris pose a threat to regional and extra-regional security—and if so, how and what specific kind of threats. This effort to disaggregate the different kinds of threats and their connections to madaris should inform the continued policy discussions about Pakistan's entire educational system. The reader alone will judge the success or failure of these attempts.

Preview of the Findings

Scant evidence supports popular claims that madaris educate a large proportion of Pakistan's full-time enrolled students. The most generous estimates put full-time madrassah enrollment at well below 10 percent, and the most conservative estimate suggests it is below 1 percent.[27] Of course, the number of children who use informal mosque schools in addition to their public or private education is certainly much higher. Unfortunately, no data provide insights into part-time utilization of religious schools. Nor does any evidence suggest that full-time madrassah market share is expanding: Andrabi et al. found that it has remained very stable since 1991 and may even be declining. Again, no data are available to illuminate trends in part-time religious school utilization. Similarly, while poorer students do make up a larger percentage of the student body at madaris than at other kinds of schools, madrassah students' socioeconomic profiles are very similar to those of students in public schools overall. Notably, madaris have a somewhat higher proportion of wealthier students than public schools: Nearly 12 percent of madrassah students come from Pakistan's wealthiest families.[28]

Studies disagree about the direct ties between madaris and militancy. My study of 140 families of slain militants in Pakistan and preliminary analysis of these data suggest that madaris were not the most important places for recruitment of militants who operated in Kashmir.[29] Less than a quarter of those militants had a madrassah background. These findings are consistent with those of numerous analysts—including Sageman, Berrebi, Bueno de Mesquita, Krueger and Malekova, Evans, and Bergen and Pandey, among others—who find little evidence that *international* terrorists have madrassah backgrounds.[30] However, suicide attackers in Afghanistan and Pakistan do seem to come from Pakistan's madaris in FATA, and sectarian militants in Pakistan are also tied to sectarian madaris.[31]

Although there may be fewer madrassah students than suggested by the popular press and they may have weak connections to militant groups, there *are* reasons for concern. A recent survey of students and teachers by Tariq Rahman suggests that madrassah students, relative to students in public and private schools, are less inclined to support equal rights for Pakistan's religious minorities and women, more likely to support mujahadeen activities in India and Kashmir, and more likely to support open war with India to resolve the Kashmir dispute. Madrassah teachers, compared both to their students and to other teachers in public and private schools, are even more inclined to support war with India and jihadi groups in Kashmir, less likely to support resolution of Kashmir through peaceful means, and generally less likely to support equal rights for Pakistan's minorities and women. Notably, public school students are more intolerant toward minorities and women and more inclined toward violent resolution of Kashmir than private school pupils, but less so than madrassah students. Public school teachers, in contrast to madrassah teachers, were more moderate than their students on Kashmir. However, with respect to minorities' and womens' rights, teachers were more intolerant than their students. Private-school students and teachers were the most moderate of the three sectors.[32]

These findings may suggest that madaris might not simply *produce* intolerant students; rather, intolerant families might *choose* madaris because they believe that madrassah teachers and administrators espouse worldviews similar to their own. (Of course, both may be true: Madaris contribute to the formation of specific norms, and parents who value those norms choose madaris for their children.) As with schoolchildren everywhere, student opinions probably reflect their home environment as much as the school environment. Switching students from madaris to private or public schools might simply result in data that suggest that public or private school students embrace values similar to those of madrassah students.

This self-selection concern is somewhat mitigated by the work of Andrabi et al., who found that madrassah utilization is less ideological than private school utilization. As mentioned above, the team found that most families (three in four) who use a madrassah for one child tend to use private or public schools for their other children. Nonetheless, research on this issue is urgently needed, because encouraging parents to opt out of the madrassah system (for example with incentives) could help discourage the production of intolerant worldviews that seem to thrive in the madaris. Or at least it could attenuate such views, holding constant the values of their families. However, before resources are devoted to this policy option, a clearer understanding is required of parental choice and the connections between educational environment and opinion formation.

A second problem associated with madaris is sectarian violence. Policy analysts, religious scholars, and Pakistani governmental officials alike share the fear that the inherently sectarian nature of madaris contributes to Pakistan's internecine strife, which claims hundreds of lives each year. The data for this assertion are limited but important. Given the gravity of sectarian violence in Pakistan, more sustained and empirically defensible analyses of such a connection are necessary.

Government officials and religious scholars suggested a third potential problem associated with Pakistani madaris: They are not producing *ulama* competent to guide a modern Islamic state. This belief has motivated support for some kinds of madrassah reform. But these interlocutors stressed that this issue is of internal importance to Pakistan and does not involve the international community.

This study found evidence that the government is making limited strides in its efforts to reform this educational sector. This success may have less to do with Islamabad's willpower than with the interests of key religious scholars. Progress has not been as fast or as comprehensive as the international community would like and has no doubt slowed because of Musharraf's domestic problems, ever-rising hostility to the United States, and the belief that Musharraf acts on behalf of the United States, not Pakistan. Notably, President Musharraf sought to implement madrassah reform *before* the events of 9/11, in recognition that doing so was in Pakistan's own interest. Those efforts have intensified—albeit episodically—since 9/11, with undulating waves of international pressure precipitated by specific regional events (the 2001–02 Indo-Pakistan military crisis, the sanctuary the Taliban enjoy in FATA and Baluchistan, and the 2006 Mumbai transit attack).

Pakistan's recent experience with a violent antigovernment madrassah in the heart of Islamabad (a women's madrassah called Jamia Hafsa associated with the radical mosque, Lal Masjid) has also underscored the need to do something about madaris that pose a threat to the country. Male and female militants of the Jamia Hafsa and the Lal Masjid rampaged through Islamabad, engaging in vigilantism for some six months before Pakistani security forces launched Operation Silence in July 2007. In the resulting confrontation as many as several hundred students died, and the madrassah was leveled in the conduct of security operations.[33]

Significant resistance to madrassah reform is coming from some madrassah administrators and educators, stemming from their financial concerns, their commitment to their madrassah's particular sectarian tradition, and their entrenched (and often valid) views about equitable treatment by the state and respect for their primary educational mission. Madrassah administrators contend that madrassah education is a specialization (no different from medical or legal education) and that they primarily produce religious scholars and others who will work in the religious educational field or with Pakistan's numerous religious political parties. They question any requirement to introduce subjects outside their specialty when, according to them, no one is asking medical schools to introduce Islamic studies into their curricula. They question why they are forced to be registered and regulated when no comparable requirement exists for private schools.[34] Increasing resistance to madrassah reform is tied to domestic politics and growing displeasure with Musharraf's domestic actions and his alliance with Washington, which spawns ever deeper acrimony. It is important to keep in mind that some within the madrassah establishment do continue to support madrassh reform. However, they want control over the process and they deny that they are undertaking these initiatives at the behest of Islamabad or Washington.

1

Contextualizing Islamic Education in Pakistan

Pakistani schools generally can be categorized as either main-stream or religious. Because Pakistanis prefer the term "worldly" to "secular," this report uses their terminology throughout.[1] Worldly education takes place in public schools (also known as "government schools" or "Urdu-medium schools") or private schools. Rightly or wrongly, private schools are sometimes referred to as "English-medium schools," even though not all private schools truly use English as the medium of instruction.

Mainstream education in Pakistan is based largely on the British educational system. Primary education includes five years (five grades) of instruction. Secondary education comprises three years of middle education (up to grade eight), and higher-secondary entails two years of high school education (up to grade ten). Postgraduate education in Pakistan begins after grade ten, after which students may pursue their F.A. (fine arts) and B.A. (baccalaureate) level studies. The more complicated schedule of religious educational programs is described elsewhere in this report. The three main forms of education (public, private, and religious) are described in some detail below.[2]

Until recent decades, formal religious education took place at institutions that provided religious education almost exclusively.[3] This general taxonomy still exists, with important exceptions. A notable one is Islamiyat (Islamic Studies), which is integrated into the government school curriculum. Although it is generally in the purview of public schools, Islamiyat is also taught at private schools that use the government's school curriculum. Some madaris have also established private and public schools that follow elite private and government school curricula respectively. Since the 1980s new schools have come into the market seeking to combine the formal madrassah curriculum with either private or public school curriculum. More generally, families can combine religious and mainstream education in various ways, through the use of both formal and informal religious schools described in chapter 2.

For example, it is common for children to memorize the Quran (Hifz-e-Quran) and thus attain the title of *hafez* before entering the mainstream school system. Students can also attend mosque schools in conjunction with their mainstream education, and many children in Pakistan receive religious instruction from a *maulvi* (religious scholar) who visits their home on a regular basis for some period of time. Religious education is clearly not confined to religious educational institutions. Thus it need not be a substitute good for worldly education and may be used to complement other kinds of education.

A comprehensive account of religious education in Pakistan requires an explanation of the larger educational context in Pakistan, to orient the reader to the variety of educational institutions and identify where religious education takes place. This chapter provides data on education and enrollment trends generally and explains variation across time, place, and socioeconomic background; presents data on educational funding and parental preferences; and includes specific information about religious education.

Varieties of Educational Institutions in Pakistan

Mainstream Educational Institutions

Mainstream education takes place at both government and private schools. In public schools the language of instruction is Urdu or another provincial language (such as Sindhi in Sindh, Baluchi in Baluchistan, and Pashto in Northwest Frontier Province).[4] The public school curriculum includes English classes that use textbooks in English. At private schools the language of instruction is usually English. Public and private educational facilities are available at all levels of education in Pakistan (primary, secondary, and postsecondary). Primary and secondary education is under the exclusive purview of the provincial government. That said, private universities are a relatively new phenomenon. Before 1991 only two recognized private universities existed, the Aga Khan University (chartered in 1983) and Lahore University of Management Sciences (established in 1985). Since 1997 the education ministry has recognized ten new private institutions.[5] Formal religious education is also available at all levels (primary, secondary, higher secondary, and postsecondary).[6]

Table 1. Total Number of Public Educational Institutions 2000—01

Gender	Makatib	Primary	Middle	High	High Secondary
Boys	13,629	59,917	6,292	5,864	403
Girls	102	42,284	5,752	2,587	276
Mixed	32	16,567	429	247	32
Totals	13,763	118,768	12,473	8,698	711

Source: Data derived from the Government of Pakistan, Ministry of Education Web site, http://www.moe.gov.pk/ (accessed April 24, 2006).

Public schools use the government-prescribed curriculum (thus the name "government schools"), and students take examinations under the authority of the relevant local examination board.[7] Educational policies, curricula, and curricular objectives are federal responsibilities, while implementation is a provincial responsibility. Islamiyat is compulsory in this stream of education up to the level of B.A. studies. Many scholars have noted that in addition to Islamiyat, the government curriculum uses Islam for a wide array of controversial ideological objectives. The government has also acknowledged that it relies on religious education as a means to construct a "democratic, tolerant, and just society as envisaged in the concept of Pakistan."[8] A comprehensive review of the Islamiyat curriculum and the application of Islam in the government curriculum is beyond the scope of this study; however, a number of fine studies, including that of A.H. Nayyar and Ahmad Salim, discuss this subject in considerable detail.[9]

Not only has the Ministry of Education included Islam in its curriculum, it also relies on mosque schools (or *makatib*, plural of *maktab*) to provide primary education and includes these schools in its inventory of primary-education establishments. According to the education ministry, in 2000–01 there were 13,763 primary religious schools (makatib) and 118,768 mainstream primary schools in Pakistan's inventory of primary educational institutions. (Table 1 provides the most recent enumeration of public educational institutions.)[10] The education ministry does not regularly collect data on madaris at present, although this may change in the near future.

It is difficult to obtain even the most basic information about the dizzying array of private schools because registration of such schools is not required in Pakistan. Therefore few comprehensive sources of information exist about them.[11] This may change in the near future; the education ministry intends to make a comprehensive survey of all schools, including public, private, and religious schools, on a district-wide basis.[12] Registered private schools are required to follow government-prescribed curricula. Thus these private schools must also teach the Islamic studies portions of the curriculum. Some private schools are accredited to prepare students for the examination of the Cambridge University Local Exams Syndicate. Private schools receive very little assistance from the government, and no information is available about them through the education ministry. Unfortunately, there is no systematic analysis of their resources and where they are obtained.

Like madaris, private schools are subject to considerable misperception. There is an enduring belief outside Pakistan that private schools are elitist, costly, and largely urban. However, many of them are not considered elitist, and economists have found that many private schools are affordable.[13] Similarly, private schools have considerable market penetration even in rural areas. Using data from Pakistan's Federal Bureau of Statistics, "Private Educational Institutions of Pakistan (PEIP) Census (March 2000)," Andrabi et al. found that nearly 26 percent of all enrolled students in Pakistan attend private schools.[14]

Similarly, recent work of Alderman et al. undermined the common assumption that "private schools which cater to the poor are exploiting low-income, often illiterate parents who are not capable of assessing if their children are learning or not." Rather, the team found that the demand for private school is related to parental perceptions of better learning opportunities. They also found that private schools are affordable in many cases and in fact provide a more efficient way of delivering higher-quality education than public school alternatives.[15]

Over the past decade several new kinds of schools, which either combine religious and worldly subjects or seek to provide worldly education in an Islamic environment, have entered the market. Several new schools combine government curricula or the elite private (Cambridge) curriculum with elements of the formal Islamic education curriculum. Some of these programs are stand-alone enterprises, while others are franchises, such as the Iqra Rozatul Itfal Trust (IRIT, a private educational foundation) chain of schools.[16]

According to administrators at a Lahore IRIT branch (Sayyadina Said Bin Zaid), prominent Deobandi religious scholars first established the trust in Karachi in 1984. The founders were concerned that students were obtaining only worldly education in public schools and madrassah students were receiving only religious education. The founders also believed that parents wanted their children to have both kinds of schooling. This claim is generally consistent with the empirical work of Mathew Nelson, whose interviews of 112 people in Rawalpindi revealed a strong preference for religious education.[17] Purportedly the trust was created only after the three founders consulted with educationalists and determined that demand existed for such a school. Some 115 IRIT schools operate throughout Pakistan.[18]

IRIT schools have separate sections for girls and boys, as well as two educational sections, the madrassah and the school section. Notably, although the founders ostensibly sought to combine religious and worldly curricula, very few of the 115 IRIT branches have the school section. It can be found only in five branches in Lahore, eight in Karachi, four in the Northern Areas, two in Peshawar, two in Rawalpindi, two in Quetta, and one each in Kasur and Gujranwala. In most cities there are separate arrangements for girls and boys; however, in some cities the school section is available only for boys.[19]

The madrassah section of IRIT schools has four levels. The first is Roza Beh, roughly equivalent to kindergarten, with students three to five years old. The second level is Roza Jim. Both Roza Beh and Roza Jim are considered pre-primary. The third level is Shoba Qaida-o-Nazira, in which students learn to read and write the Arabic alphabet. On completing this level students begin the fourth level, where they memorize the Quran (Shoba-e-Hifz-e-Quran). This is generally four years long but ultimately depends on the student's ability to successfully memorize the Quran. Most students complete this stage by the time they are ten to twelve years old. Once the student completes this phase of study, he or she embarks on the "school phase." According to administrators at the branch I visited, about 90 percent of students who complete the madrassah portion of the program continue on to the school program.[20]

The school section begins with a one-year course, during which students purportedly master the complete content of the government curriculum for grades one through five.[21] After this preparatory course, students begin studying the regular sixth-grade subjects and continue until matriculation. (In Pakistan students obtain matriculation certificates by completing ten years of education and passing an examination. "Matric" qualification is a prerequisite for many jobs in Pakistan, as well as admission to colleges and universities.) IRIT branches with school sections follow the curriculum of the relevant provincial board of intermediate and secondary education with which they are registered.[22] Students sit for the appropriate exams as determined by the provincial educational board. IRIT schools do accept outside students, provided they are hafez and are willing to take the one-year preparatory course. Students seeking to opt out of the preparatory year must successfully test into the desired class level.

It will take some time to determine how IRIT students perform across the country or even to evaluate the grandiose claims of its administrators. Is it really possible to master the materials of five grade levels in one year, as they claim? However, at the Lahore branch I visited, 100 percent of their students successfully passed their board exams. In Karachi, IRIT schools have produced nine graduating cohorts, and reportedly their students have also faired very well on the textbook board exams, with some students testing with distinction.[23] Reflecting the popularity of IRIT schools, other private educational trusts have adopted similar names (Iqra Medina, Iqra Ryazul Itfa, Iqra Jannatul Itfa) and seek to accomplish similar goals.

The Arqam Academy is a nonprofit organization that, like the IRIT chain, aims to produce students who are "fully knowledgeable about [the] modern world as well as becoming a true hafez of the Holy Quran."[24] Arqam has a two-year kindergarten section and a primary-school section that goes up to the fifth grade. In addition to memorization of the Quran, Arqam teaches English, general knowledge, math and science.[25] Other Islamic-education enterprises (such as Al Huda) impart Islamic education exclusively but target disparate markets, such as housewives, slum dwellers, graduates of mainstream education, prisons, hospitals (for those grieving loved ones), working women, and students currently at colleges and universities.[26]

The IRIT and similar systems are important and have a nationwide presence to varying degrees, but Nizamat-i-Islami oversees some 2,000 private schools throughout Pakistan. These schools are often associated with medical clinics that provide free or subsidized medical care to localities.[17] Nizamat-i-Islami is the education office of the Islamist political party Jamaat-i-Islami. Moreover, Jamaat-i-Islami members may privately establish schools beyond the purview of the Nizamat-i-Islami. For instance, the Green Crescent Trust operates dozens of such schools in the southern province of Sindh.[28] This suggests that Jamaat-i-Islami private schools may considerably exceed 2,000. These independent schools raise funds locally to build and establish private schools, recruit and train teachers, and educate students according to Jamaat-i-Islami ideology. Jamaat-i-Islami members assert that these schools "infuse the government curriculum with Islamic studies to favorably influence young people toward Jamaat-i-Islami ideology."[29] They further claim that their students take national government examinations and pursue higher studies in both public and private colleges and universities.[30]

Darul Uloom Islamiya (Islamabad) is a "model boys' madrassah" and an important example of an institution that combines both worldly and religious subjects with reported success in both areas. Founded in 1986 and registered in 2000 as a trust, it offers several levels of instruction. The first and most elementary level is Hifz-e-Quran, and this typically takes two to three years to complete. It is followed by Marhala Mutavassata, comprising three years' instruction and covering translation of the Quran, Hadith, jurisprudence, grammar, Arabic, and other religious subjects. Simultaneously students learn worldly subjects associated with the sixth through eighth grades of the Federal Textbook Board (Islamabad). The third level, Marhala Kuliya, is a four-year course at whose end students can sit the exam for their faculty of arts degree from the Punjab University, as well as their Thanviya-e-Khassah degree from the Deobandi testing board. (Both this degree and the board are described below.) The final level is Marhala Alimiyah, which is two years long and aims to produce students who pass tests for the highest madrassah degree, Alimiyah (also described below).

Administrators of this school believe that their contribution is their simultaneous instruction of worldly and religious scholars and their ability to produce students with college degrees as well as religious certificates. As with IRIT schools and other such enterprises, Darul Uloom has produced only a few graduating classes, and so it is too early to assess claims of success advanced by these school administrators.[31]

In addition to schools run by educational trusts that seek to combine elements of the madrassah curriculum and worldly subjects, several madaris have established private English-medium schools or public schools, so named because they use the government curriculum and do not explicitly teach Islamic subjects, apart from the government-prescribed Islamic studies.[32] This type is distinct from IRIT or Darul Uloom in that students at these schools do not receive any training that would qualify them for religious certificates. Madrassah administrators explain that their comparative advantage in imparting worldly education is that they do so in an "Islamic environment." In their view, this appeals to parents who desire worldly education for their children's successful social advancement as well as the inculcation of prized religious and moral values. An excellent example of such an enterprise is Kher-ul-Madaris in Multan, which has opened free public schools and an elite, fee-based private school. The fee structure at this private madrassah-operated school is comparable to that of leading private schools.[33]

According to madrassah administrators, think-tank analysts, government officials, and religious scholars I interviewed, this is a growing trend, with several madaris establishing such schools in recent years. Some—but not all—madaris subsidize these enterprises for parents who cannot afford the fees.[34] Madrassah administrators explained during fieldwork for this study that these schools appeal to middle-class and upper-middle-class parents who want their children to receive a high-quality worldly education in an Islamic environment. To date, there have been no comprehensive studies of this phenomenon. However, Dietrich Reetz has begun a project to better understand the proliferation of hybrid educational systems increasingly available in the Pakistani market.[35]

The government also runs various English-medium schools, some of which teach subjects in Urdu as well as English, for its own dependents.

Offering this kind of educational enterprise is the military, which controls eighty-eight federal English-medium schools in cantonments where military personnel receive subsidized education for their dependents. In addition, some prominent private schools are administered under the auspices of the armed forces and their various foundations.[36] For instance, in 2003–04 the army ran 120 schools and colleges. The air force and navy operated twenty-seven schools and twenty-nine colleges in the same year. According to data collected by Rahman, the army's Fauji Foundation runs eighty-eight secondary and four higher-secondary schools. Although these schools are very affordable for Fauji Foundation beneficiaries, they charge civilian students significantly more. The navy's Baharia Foundation and the air force's Shaheen Foundation also run schools for their qualified dependents.[37] Rahman concludes from these data that "the armed forces have entered the field of English-medium, elitist education and generally provided cheap English-medium schooling to their own dependents."[38]

The military is not the only governmental body offering quality education to its own members. Numerous other state agencies, including the Water and Power Development Authority (WAPDA), the Customs Department, the Pakistan Railways, the Telephone Foundation, and the police, run English-medium schools. These schools have an affordable fee structure for their employees and are open to the public at higher cost. English is generally the medium of instruction (a highly prized feature that is thought to bring success in the labor market); but these schools reportedly are highly variable in the quality of education they offer.[39]

An examination of the various kinds of government-sponsored private schools (the "elite public schools") suggests that the government is generally able to provide a wide array of quality institutions for its own while seemingly unable or unwillingto rehabilitate the public school system. It is difficult to escape Rahman's fundamental conclusions:

> … English-medium schooling can be bought either by the elite of wealth or that of power. And this has not happened through market forces but has been brought about by the functionaries or institutions of the state itself. Indeed, the state has invested heavily in creating a parallel system of education for the elite, especially the elite that would presumably run elitist state institutions in the future. This leads

to the conclusion that the state does not trust its own system of education and spends public funds to create and maintain the parallel, elitist
system of schooling.[40]

This state of affairs disconcerts analysts such as Rahman because the
military has ruled Pakistan directly and indirectly for most of Pakistan's
history and yet has done little to provide education for Pakistan's masses
that is comparable to the system for the children of serving and retired
military personnel. More generally, critics of the military see this as yet
another example of its providing for its own welfare while doing little to
advance the welfare of the country's citizenry.

Religious Educational Institutions

The medium of instruction at religious schools is generally Urdu or
Arabic, although some religious educational programs for foreigners
use English or Arabic. As with mainstream education, there are several
levels of formal Islamic education in Pakistan. Other informal varieties,
such as Dars-e-Quran (Quran study circles), often take place in private
homes. Islamic scholars and organizations have developed products and
resources to help people in their studies of the Quran in these informal
environments, and these resources are accessible via the Internet.[41]
Informal Islamic education is not systemized by levels and happens in a
more ad hoc manner. This kind of education is akin to Bible study
groups that may be familiar to readers in the United States.

However, Islamic education imparted at formal religious institutions
is systematized, even though the specific duration and content of education at each level may vary with the sectarian orientation of the madrassah in question and the extent to which it has augmented its curriculum
with mainstream subjects. Thus conditions may vary. The following
schedule is based on a standard, seventeen-year, formal Islamic education program.

- The first level is Ibtedai (primary or elementary), where only the
  Quran is taught. This level covers the early five-year period of education that is generally equivalent to the primary-school level in the
  mainstream educational sector.

- The second stage is Mutawassitah, or intermediary. It is generally
  three years long and comparable to the middle-school level at main-

stream schools. It may include elements of a specialized curriculum to produce religious scholars called ulama.

- The third through sixth levels are each two years long. At this stage students begin the Alim course curriculum. Often called Dars-i-Nizami, it is modified according to the particular sectarian affiliation of the madrassah in question. Madaris of different sectarian affiliations will teach different versions of the curriculum. Sometimes this eight-year, four-stage program is referred to as *fauqani*. Or it may be called the "Alim course," in reference to the final certificate or degree (*sanad*). The first of the four stages is Thanviyah-e-Ammah, followed by Thanviyah-e-Khassah. The next two stages, Aaliyah and Alimiyah, are considered advanced. When students complete the Alimiyah level, they have completed the Dars-i-Nizami curriculum. This degree is recognized by some bodies in Pakistan as an M.A. in two subjects (Islamic studies and Arabic). A person with this degree is an alim.

- The final stage of religious study is Takmeel. Comparable to post-graduate studies, it can be one year or more long and comprises various specialized fields of study.[42]

Broadly, these kinds of education take place in full or in part in two kinds of formal Islamic educational facilities: the maktab and the madrassah. The pre-primary and primary (Ibtedai) religious school is "the mosque school" or maktab. Maktab classes may be held in a mosque, in a courtyard of houses, or even underneath a tree. Informally run and ubiquitous in Pakistan, they teach children between five and nine (the age of a third-grade student). This comparison to the third grade is only hypothetical because makatib generally do not teach worldly subjects.[43]

In fact, maktab educational offerings are very limited and cover what are considered to be foundational subjects, such as Nazira-e-Quran (reading the Quran) and Hifz-e-Quran (memorizing the Quran). Makatib do not impart elements of the Alim course.[44] Sometimes institutions that appear to be makatib teach subjects that are generally taught in the lower levels of formal madrassah education. However, most of the administrators of Islamic schools I interviewed suggest that it is uncommon for smaller, local makatib to teach more rigorous secondary subjects; those that do may be satellites of madaris. For example, a famous Karachi madrassah, Jamiat ul Uloom I Islamiyyah (also known as Allama Sayyad Muhammad Yousuf Banuri Town), has fifteen branches in addition to the central madrassah. The full madrassah curriculum (Alim course or Dars-i-Nizami) is offered at only five of the branches. The remaining branches teach reading and memorization of the Quran. Because these are branches of Banuri Town, they may be classified as madaris rather than makatib, even though they offer only primary Islamic education. On completing their primary education, students may transfer to another branch where the Alim course is available. Another reason they may be considered madaris is that they have some students who live in hostels at the branches. Many—if not most—madaris have residential facilities.[45]

Notwithstanding the similarities with madrassah satellite schools, makatib tend to be smaller than madaris and educate fewer than thirty students. Maktab students do not study at the maktab fulltime, and because maktab classes are generally held in the morning and afternoon, children may also attend mainstream schools. Makatib are for local students and do not have hostels and other residential facilities. Madaris, unlike makatib, are educational institutions based on the Islamic sciences (Quran, Hadith, *fiqh*, theology, Arabic languages, and other subjects) at various levels.

In contrast to makatib, madaris generally provide secondary education; some provide higher secondary education and even postsecondary training. They tend to educate several hundred and even thousands of students. Study programs at the larger madaris are almost always full time. Madaris also vary widely in class size and student-to-teacher ratios. Many, but not all, madaris have residential facilities for nonlocal students, while some madaris are for day scholars only.[46] The sina qua non distinguishing madaris from makatib is the Alim course or Dars-i-Nizami curriculum, which madaris teach in full or in part, depending on the resources of the madrassah. (See the sample Deobandi curriculum in appendix A.) Madaris can be categorized as *jamia* (or colleges) and *darul uloom* (universities), which sometimes offer postgraduate specialization, depending on faculty availability. Because not all madaris teach the full curriculum, students may need to study at several madaris to obtain the highest religious degree offered.[47]

The Pakistani government has relied on the religious educational institutions to achieve its domestic aims in its various five-year plans (which are not always released every five years, despite the name). In 1970 the government released its "New Education Policy," in which it acknowledged the role of makatib and madaris in providing education. It suggested that West Pakistan had nearly 700 maktab-type institutions and a few higher-level madaris at that time.[48]

Following the breakup of Pakistan in 1971, the government put forth its education policy of 1972–80. This document gave religious institutions the mandate to operate under the government's guidelines for private institutions. The National Education Policy and Implementation Programme of 1979 explicitly articulated the role of the makatib and advocated making the Quran accessible to Pakistan's masses. Throughout the 1970s, the government sponsored openings of new mosque schools and strengthened existing makatib. The 1979 policy advocated opening makatib in areas where no primary schools existed instead of building public primary schools.[49] The explicit support for makatib probably explains why the education ministry includes them in its tally of primary educational institutions, even though these makatib do not actually offer any mainstream primary subjects.

The National Education Policy document of 1992 continued this well-established trend of identifying the need for Islamic education and Islamic educational institutions. It expressed dissatisfaction with science and technology training, deeming it insufficient for the intellectual and moral development of young people. Instead it declared, "Islam was the way to produce a truly egalitarian Muslim society."[50] By the 1990s the number of makatib had increased substantially. The National Education Policy 1998–01 concluded that religious and modern schools should be integrated and pledged to provide financial and other incentives for integration.[51]

Educational Enrollment and Attainment Trends

Pakistan continues to have low school-enrollment rates and educational attainment, high illiteracy, and persistent gaps between male and female education. While this study focuses on Islamic education, it is useful to understand the overall educational landscape in Pakistan. A discussion follows of enrollment and attainment in Pakistan and the determinants of dominant trends, as well as regional and temporal differences and differences in enrollment across educational sectors.

Overall Enrollment and Attainment

Enrollment data for Pakistan are somewhat contradictory. According to data provided for 2001 by a Pakistani research institute, the Social Policy and Development Center (SPDC), Pakistan's overall primary enrollment rate was 74.2 percent. The primary school rate is defined by the number of students enrolled in primary-level classes (one to five) as a percentage of the population of children aged five to nine. However, the female enrollment rate of 63.5 percent compares poorly to the figure of 83.9 percent for males. The overall secondary-school enrollment rate for all students was only 28.4 percent—23.37 percent for girls and 33.1 percent for boys. Secondary enrollment rate is defined by the number of students enrolled in classes six through ten as a percentage of the population aged ten to fourteen. However, the United Nations Development Index for 2003 gives a considerably grimmer picture, with a much lower net primary-enrollment rate of 59 percent and combined enrollment ratio for primary, secondary, and tertiary schools of 35 percent. Likewise, 2003 adult and youth literacy rates are low at 48.7 percent and 64.5 percent respectively, with females lagging behind males in both groups.[52]

Overall educational attainment is also low. In 2002 the Population Council completed a nationally representative survey of Pakistani youth. According to that study, the average years of schooling completed were 6.2 classes for male respondents and 3.5 classes for females. These figures are low because they include youths who never attended any school at all. In fact, 36 percent of respondents claimed they had never attended school, with a large gender difference of 46 percent for females and 16 percent for males.[53]

Although the overall educational attainment in Pakistan is not high, the retention rate conditional on school entry is somewhat more encouraging. According to a 2001 study of household schooling decisions in rural Pakistan (using data collected from fourteen villages of the Faisalabad and Attock districts in the Punjab and eleven villages from the Dir districts in Northwest Frontier Province), the team of Sawada and Lokshin found that families appear to pick educational "winners" and make efforts to keep them in school once they decide to enroll these children. According to their survey, although the average number of years of schooling for girls in their sample was only 1.6 years, the average years of schooling for girls who entered primary school was six years. The average schooling for boys was 6.6 years, while the conditional average was 8.8 years. In other words, the overall average is low because many children never enter the educational system. But years of schooling conditional upon entry are substantially higher. This "picking the winner" effect is substantially higher for girls than for boys. The authors also found significant regional differences: Surveyed families in the NWFP were substantially less likely to enroll their daughters than families from the Punjab.[54]

Enrollment across Educational Sectors

Limited data address the market share of enrolled students in the three main educational sectors in Pakistan: public (government) schools, private schools, and religious schools (madaris). The PIHS, the nationally representative survey of Pakistani households, permits analysis of market share while acknowledging the various data caveats mentioned earlier. Analyses of PIHS data suggest that overall, madrassah education is low: 0.9 percent of all full-time students. In contrast, government schools educate 73 percent of students, and private schools educate 26 percent. There is some variation between rural and urban areas. Madaris capture only 0.7 percent of the market in urban areas, whereas government schools capture 62 percent and private schools 37 percent. In rural areas madaris capture 1.1 percent of student enrollment, and public and private schools educate 83 percent and 17 percent of students, respectively. (These data are given in table 2.) Despite these gross enrollment trends, variation is considerable according to socioeconomic status of the student and by geographical location of the household, as described below. There is comparatively less variation across time, despite popular accounts of madrassah expansion.[55]

Table 2. Distribution of Primary Enrollment (Percent), 2001

Sector	Urban	Rural	Total
Government	62.4	81.8	73.0
Private School	36.9	17.0	26.1
Madrassah	0.7	1.1	0.9
Total	100	100	100

Source: Derived from analyses of PIHS 2001 data available in Social Policy and Development Center, *Social Development in Pakistan Annual Review 2002-03—The State of Education,* 157; http://www.spdc-pak.com/publications/sdip2003.asp.

Enrollment Trends by Socioeconomic Status

Again using data from the most recent wave of the PIHS (2001), the Social Policy and Development Center examined socioeconomic status of students enrolled in three types of schools (madrassah, public, and private). They found that among those enrolled in madaris (0.9 percent overall), the largest fraction (43 percent) were from households with annual incomes of less than Rs.50,000 ($865). The next largest share came from households with annual incomes between Rs.50,000 ($865) and Rs.100,000 ($1,730). Nearly 16 percent came from households with annual incomes between Rs.100,000 ($1,730) and 250,000 ($4,325). Another 12 percent came from households with annual incomes above Rs.250,000 ($4,325). (See table 3.) This is somewhat similar to the pattern observed for Urdu-medium public schools, which account for 73 percent of total primary enrollments. It is useful to note that that the same wave of PIHS data suggests that the average annual household income was Rs.93,684 ($1,620). Thus, Rs.50,000 ($865) is about half the national average household income.[56]

However, average incomes are not the best benchmarks because they are distorted by high- and low-income values. For this reason, it is useful

Table 3. Distribution of School Enrollment by Education System and Income (Percent)

Annual Income (Rs)	Elite Private Schools	Non-Elite Private Schools	Public Schools	Madaris
Overall				
<50,000	0.0	12.3	27.2	24.6
50,000-100,000	1.5	35.1	44.7	40.0
100,000-250,000	32.1	41.4	24.9	20.0
>250,000	66.4	11.2	3.2	15.4
Urban				
<50,000	0.0	38.7	51.5	61.9
50,000-100,000	0.0	35.9	32.6	19.0
100,000-250,000	33.3	19.1	12.4	11.1
>250,000	66.7	6.3	3.6	7.9
Rural				
<50,000	0.0	18.9	40.4	43.0
50,000-100,000	1.5	35.3	38.1	29.7
100,000-250,000	32.1	35.8	18.1	15.6
>250,000	66.4	10.0	3.4	11.7

Source: PIHS 2001, compiled and published by the Social Policy and Development Center, 160; http://www.spdc-pak.com/publications/sdip2003.asp.

to use quintiles to divide families by income. Quintiles for this wave of PIHS data are presented in table 4. The cutoff point for annual income for the first (lowest) quintile of household income is Rs.52,692 ($911). This means that a fifth of surveyed families in the PIHS have

Table 4. Monthly and Estimated Annual Income by Quintile

Period	Total	1st Quintile	2nd Quintile	3rd Quintile	4th Quintile	5th Quintile
Monthly Income	7,167	4,391	5,224	5,943	6,722	11,360
Estimated Yearly Income	86,004	52,692	62,688	71,316	80,664	136,320

Source: Federal Bureau of Statistics, Government of Pakistan, Islamabad. Household *Integrated Economic Survey Round 4: 2001–02.* Table 11, Percentage Distribution of Monthly Household Income: By Source and Quintiles, 2001–02," April 2003; http://www.statpak.gov.pk/epts./fbs/statistics/hies0102/hies0102t11.pdf (accessed April 25, 2006).

annual incomes at or below this level. The cutoff for the fifth quintile is Rs.136,320 ($2,358). Thus 20 percent of the sample of PIHS households have annual incomes of Rs.136,320 ($2,358) or greater. Breaking down annual income into quintiles demonstrates that the vast majority of Pakistani households (60 percent) earn between Rs.52,692 ($911) and Rs.136,320 ($2,358).

Presenting income by quintiles affects the interpretation of the information provided in the tabulation of the PIHS data in table 3 in several ways. First, the tabulations demonstrate that in each stream of education there are different distributions of student socioeconomic background, although the distributions for madrassah and public school students are quite similar. However, the cutoff points—Rs.50,000 ($865), Rs.100,000 ($1,730), Rs.250,000 ($4,325)—are not terribly helpful; they obfuscate the extent to which madrassah students are not exclusively poor. In fact, annual incomes of Rs.250,000 ($4,325) are well over the cutoff point for the fifth quintile, and those families are exceedingly well-off by Pakistani standards. Second, this exercise suggests that although the concentration of poorer students is not surprising (from households in the first quintile), it is surprising that nearly 12 percent come from the wealthiest households in Pakistan (well above the cutoff for the fifth quintile). Third, 27 percent of madrassah students come from households that straddle the fourth and fifth quintiles and are still relatively well-off families, with incomes above Rs.100,000 ($1,730).

Taken together, these recast observations do not undermine the SPDC's general thesis of distributional differences across the sectors by income. The asymmetry between elite private schools (attended mostly by the richest families) and madaris (attended by lower- and middle-class families) is noteworthy. But this exercise also illuminates that madaris students do come from families in the middle and higher quintiles of household income, something that has not been generally understood. Unfortunately, relying upon problematic measures like averages obscures this fact.

The Andrabi team sought to explore in greater detail the determinants of parental choice to enroll children in madaris as well as public and private schools. They wanted to understand how madrassah households (a household with at least one child enrolled in a madrassah) differ from non-madrassah households (a household with no children in a madrassah).

Because madrassah enrollment is a rare phenomenon and sophisticated analysis of differences across households would require a large sample size of madrassah households, the Andrabi team used data from a household census they had conducted in 2003, surveying all households in selected villages in the Punjab. This selection is defensible and even appropriate, at least in part, because the Punjab has the most madaris in Pakistan, reflecting the fact that the Punjab is the most populated state with the highest population density. (The inventory of schools of all varieties logically is related to the number of school-age children, which in turn is correlated with population.)[57] According to 2000 data compiled by Saleem Mansoor Khalid (and presented in table 6), the Punjab accounted for the largest fraction of madaris in Pakistan (3,153 out of 6,741).[58]

Andrabi et al. were interested in knowing whether madrassah utilization was ideologically driven. Their study suggested that madrassah utilization did not appear to be ideological in nature, although they found evidence that use of private schools might be. Moreover, they found that among all "madrassah households," only 24 percent could be classified as "all-madrassah" households. In other words, most madrassah households also used other kinds of schools for their children. Almost 50 percent of madrassah households use madaris and public schools; another

28 percent have at least one child in a private school.[59] If madrassah choice were primarily ideological for most madrassah households, families probably would not use madaris in conjunction with mainstream schools, often with direct and opportunity costs imposed upon the families. Rather, it seems as if most families are selecting particular educational streams for various children, which buttresses work presented earlier that families pick winners. By way of caution, it should be noted that this finding in no way precludes the possibility that some families do select madaris for their children for specifically ideological reasons. Recall that one quarter of madrassah households *do* use madaris for all of their children.

The Andrabi team did find an association between low-income households and madrassah enrollment and between less-educated heads of household and madrassah enrollment, but these associations were weak. They found that the strongest difference between madrassah and non-madrassah households is their proximity to a private school. To explain the reasons for this unexpected finding, they explored three parental choice scenarios in their data: 1) localities where both private and public schools are present; 2) localities where either a public or a private school exists; and 3) localities where neither non-madrassah option is available.

Three findings emerged from this exercise:

1. In settlements with both public and private options, private-school market share increased with income. However, 30 percent of the poor families still sent their children to private schools. In these localities madrassah share is still less than 1 percent, with no difference in utilization between poor and rich families.

2. In settlements with either a public or private school, they observed patterns similar to those described above.

3. In localities with no public or private schools, enrollment patterns were very different. The largest difference was the choice to enroll at all. Where there were no alternatives, families were more likely to simply exit education rather than send their children to a madrassah. The drop in enrollment was striking, falling from 70 percent to 40 percent among the poor and from 87 percent to 68 percent among the rich.[60]

Table 5. Pakistan's Madrassah Enrollment: Different Sources

Data Source	Madrassah Enrollments	Madrassah as a Percentage of All Students Enrolled
Census of Population-1998	159,225	0.70
PIHS-1991	151,546	0.78
PIHS-1998	178,436	0.74
PIHS-2001	176,061	0.70

Source: Tabulations presented in Tahir Andrabi et al., "Religious School Enrollment in Pakistan," 33.

Essentially, in rural localities households first decide whether or not they will enroll a child, followed by a private-public decision with the possible option of madrassah enrollment. When non-madrassah schools are not available, families are more likely to simply drop out of the educational market rather than send their children to madaris, although evidence in the study indicates that madaris enjoy increased market share among the poor in such localities.[61]

Madrassah Enrollment Trends across Time

Using the national data from both the 1998 Pakistan Census and three waves of the PIHS, the Andrabi team looked at enrollment trends across time. Because actual numbers of school enrollments scale with the size of the school-age population, comparing school enrollments per se across public, private, and religious schools is not useful. (Over time, one would expect actual numbers of school enrollments to increase because the population of school-age children is increasing.) For this reason, one needs to examine relative measures of enrollment that take into consideration the size of the enrolled population. Andrabi et al. do so by using a measure of the relative market share of madaris, public schools, and private schools. Market share is obtained by dividing the number of full-time students in a particular kind of school by the total number of children enrolled fulltime. Using this measure, they found that full-time madrassah enrollment is very low—less than 1 percent of total full-time enrollments—across Pakistan. (See table 5.) But this analysis demonstrates that madrassah market share (madrassah students as a fraction of all enrollments) was stable—and perhaps even declining—between 1991 (0.78 percent) and 2001 (0.7 percent). These data cast doubt on the pervasive belief that madaris' penetration has deepened in recent decades.

Geographical Variation in Madrassah Enrollment Trends

Although national rates of madrassah enrollment appear to be less than 1 percent, there is enormous geographical variation in madrassah market share. Data from the 2001 PIHS (presented in table 2) suggests distributional differences between enrollments in school sectors for rural and urban residents. Nationally 73 percent of enrolled students are in public schools, but 81.8 percent are enrolled in this sector in rural areas, compared to 62.4 percent in urban areas. Private school enrollment patterns are the reverse. The national average is 26.1 percent, but in urban areas 36.9 percent are enrolled in private schools, compared to 17 percent in rural areas. Madrassah enrollments are low in both urban and rural areas (0.7 percent and 1.1 percent, respectively).[62]

Andrabi's study provides considerable information on geographical variation in enrollment trends for madaris. Using data from the 1998 Census, the Andrabi team found that the top ten districts in terms of madrassah market share are all in the Pashto-speaking belt along the Pakistan-Afghanistan border in Baluchistan and Northwest Frontier Province. Using a measure of "extreme madrassah enrollment," defined as a district with madrassah market share greater than 2 percent, they found fourteen of Pakistan's 102 districts qualified. These districts were Lasbela, Kharan, Kalata, Kohlu, Loralai, Kila Abdullah, Khob, Pishin, Hangu, Zarak, Lower Dir, Shangla, Buner and Chitral. With the exception of Lasbela, in Baluchistan abutting Karachi, all of these high-intensity madrassah districts are along the Afghanistan-Pakistan border. Notably, in Pishin (in Baluchistan, near the Afghan border, Kandahar region) madrassah market share was 9 percent. It is very important to note that the team could not evaluate the important areas of FATA because census data were not available for FATA.[63]

Determinants of School Enrollment and Retention

Sawada and Lokshin's econometric inquiry into parental choice also cast much-needed light on household schooling decisions, including the choice to enroll children in school in the first place and to continue their studies once enrolled. One of the most important determinants of school enrollment and retention for girls is school supply. Their study did not find a similarly strong connection between school supply and enrollment for boys. This finding strongly suggests that a lack of primary and secondary schools in the student's locality impedes girls' education, although this supply-side effect is not as severe for boys. It supports the conclusions of Andrabi et al. that a dearth of mainstream schools compels families to opt out of the education market altogether. A second factor is the availability of female teachers. Even if a girls' school is located near the home, the chronic shortage of women teachers constrains female educational access. In one study examining rural female students in Pakistan, Chaudhary and Chaudhary found that even with nonmonetary and monetary incentives (such as scholarships), girls would attend only if the schools were opened with female teachers in each village.[64]

Not only are girls' school accessibility and appropriate female teachers associated with increased probability of a girl being enrolled, these factors increase the likelihood of her continued enrollment. The stark supply-side constraints for female education are in large measure rooted in parental and family concerns about girls' honor (*izzat*) and, by extension, the honor of the family. Families are hesitant to educate daughters if the local school is far from the home, and these concerns are compounded by the fact that most families in Pakistan cannot afford private and secure transportation for their daughters. For example, girls may be harassed by males, have inappropriate access to males, or engage in other activities to which the family objects or which will socially disgrace the family.[65]

Sawada and Lokshin also found that parental decisions not to enroll their children were based on their perception that the local school had low-quality teachers. If the school quality is low, parents may conclude that the direct costs (for schools, uniforms, and materials) as well as the opportunity costs (foregone domestic production and compensated child labor) of educating their children outweigh the perceived current and future benefits of the education available. Sawada and Lokshin also found that the level of the father's and mother's education was positively correlated to child attainment. In other words, the more educated the parents are, the more educated their children will be, all else equal. Sawada and Lokshin found that physical assets owned by households were positively associated with child enrollment and attainment and that negative income shocks (events resulting in unexpected loss of income) discourage continuing school attendance. Negative health shocks (such as unexpected illness, death, or injury) in the household also contributed to school dropout, at least partly because serious illness or a death in the family imposes both financial and nonfinancial hardship. These findings suggest that families with greater financial wherewithal are better able than families without such resources to take the risk that educating children will have future payoffs.[66]

While the state cannot immediately influence demand for education and the concomitant determinants of parental choice, this research strongly suggests the importance of supply-side interventions such as increasing the supply of schools or teachers. Obviously, Pakistan's failure to increase female educational enrollment and attainment perpetuates the restriction on the supply of high-quality female teachers, which in turn discourages families from sending their daughters to school. Pakistan needs to break this negative cycle by dramatically expanding the supply of girls' schools and creating important incentives to encourage the production of female teachers to address these interrelated problems.

These studies yield numerous insights into parental choice with respect to religious educational institutions. Although mainstream schools in rural areas may be subject to teacher and school supply-side constraints, makatib and madaris are widely available. To the extent that madaris provide financial incentives to buffer families against income, asset, and health shocks, their availability can encourage parents to take a higher risk in educating their children. The wisdom of the prescribed policy of reforming madaris may be misplaced if the objective is to create citizens of a modern state who can contribute to the economy that Pakistan seeks to develop. Given the inherent advantages of madaris in terms of physical location and ability to provide extensive welfare services to children and their families, further investments in this sector may pose substantial opportunity costs in that those outlays may preclude necessary expenditures for developing the mainstream educational sector while increasing the relevant advantage of madaris in the educational market.

However, there are at least two countervailing considerations. First, evidence shows that parents who choose Islamic education do so because they actively prefer it.[67] A second observation, made by Andrabi et al., is that even in localities without public or private schools, in contrast with better-off counterparts, poorer households do tend to use the madrassah. Nonetheless, madrassah utilization is still a rare choice. Families are more likely to exit the system than use the madrassah.

Taken together these two conclusions suggest that many families that do select madaris for their children do so not because they are compelled to (due to poverty) but out of preference. Family use of madaris is therefore not exclusively ideological. Thus it may not be the case that families value the restrictive and intolerant worldview of the madrassah. Rather, they may value the religious benefits that they believe accrue from religious education and anticipate that such instruction may help their children become good Muslims.[68] It is far from obvious how madrassah or educational reform will influence these parental choices, at least partly because there is much to learn yet about parental choice between madaris and mainstream schools.

The meaningful effort to shape the demand for education among Pakistan's parents cannot be accomplished simply through government intervention to increase the supply of schools and teachers. Such intervention should reflect parental preferences in terms of the quality of education and what parents understand the determinants of quality to be. For example, are parental decisions to educate influenced by the perceived reward for education in the labor market? Is the availability of Islamic religious instruction a mark of quality? Does education affect marriage market possibilities for their children and, by extension, the family? Effective educational policy requires a solid understanding of parental choice. At present virtually all policy recommendations from the United States and Pakistani governments regarding Pakistan's mainstream and religious educational systems are ad hoc and without empirical basis. This is not a prescription for success over any period.

Funding Trends for Islamic Education

Pakistan has endured sustained criticism of its inadequate funding for public education across the board. Whereas the nation spent 4.8 percent of its gross domestic product (GDP) on its military in 2003 (the most recent year for which data are available), Pakistan's public health and education expenditures are among the lowest in the world as a proportion of GDP.[69] And education expenditures are shrinking. Pakistan has the ignominious distinction of being one of only seven countries that spend less than 2 percent of GDP on education, according to statistics in the most recent Human Development Report of the United Nations Development Program.[70] The Pakistani government is keenly aware that its macroeconomic growth cannot be sustained without simultaneous investments in Pakistan's human capital. That said, most of the numerous past efforts to reform Pakistan's variegated educational system have had little measurable success.[71]

The most recent effort undertaken by the Musharraf government is Education Sector Reform (ESR), launched in January 2002. One of its major objectives was development of a more "secular" system to stave off the ever-mounting international pressure to counter Islamist extremism after the September 11 terrorist attacks. Elements of these reforms (including madrassah reform) again came to the fore following the July 7, 2005, terrorist attacks in London and the ostensible links between the terrorists and Pakistan's madaris. (None of the most ambitious claims about the London terrorists receiving training in Pakistan's madaris has been substantiated.)

Another important feature of ESR is madrassah reform, through which the government seeks to "mainstream" the madaris by encouraging them to expand their curriculum and enhance the quality of education. To accomplish these objectives, ESR will provide grants, salaries to teachers, and the cost of textbooks, teacher training, and equipment. ESR's goals include the introduction of "formal subjects, English, math, social/Pakistan studies, and general science" at the primary, middle, and secondary levels, "while English, economics, Pakistan studies, and computer science will be introduced at the intermediate level."[72]

In January 2002 Musharraf's government launched a five-year, $113 million plan to finance the introduction of these formal subjects to the madrassah curriculum by madaris that were willing to do so. Both Pakistani officials and madrassah administrators I interviewed contended that very few established madaris had taken these funds. Both kinds of interviewees claimed that some new madaris had been established explicitly to take these monies, and both said they were not credible institutions of religious instruction.

In addition the government set up three model madaris in Karachi, Sukkur, and Islamabad in 2005. It was the intention of the Ministry for Religious Affairs, Zakat, and Ushr (henceforth religious affairs ministry) to establish model madaris in each of Pakistan's four provinces, in addition to the federal area of Islamabad. However, as of August 2007 only those three had been established. The Islamabad madrassah is exclusively for girls. Government officials say the Islamabad school initially attracted much interest, with more applicants than available seats. There is no further information about the model madaris in Sukkur and Karachi.[73]

Reliable data on funding for religious schools, aside from general government allocations, are unavailable. Madrassah administrators I interviewed insisted that they were funded by private domestic philanthropists. Independent and think-tank analysts, as well as governmental analysts, share this view. However, some of the larger madaris do appear to be profitable family enterprises, and many include private ventures that subsidize madrassah activities. Jamia Binoria SITE of Karachi exemplifies this cross-subsidy phenomenon. It is a twelve-acre enclave with numerous private-sector enterprises, including family restaurants, student canteens, wedding lawns, bakeries, and other businesses that provide income for the madrassah. Some madaris receive substantial in-kind goods, such as food and kitchen supplies. Madrassah administrators interviewed for this study denied taking *zakat*; many even claimed that their students were not receiving zakat, although there are reasons to discount this claim. (As discussed below, students receive zakat if they apply to their local zakat board.)

The religious affairs ministry does provide zakat to students (who may attend any kind of institution), conditional upon certification by the local zakat board attesting to their eligibility. The religious affairs ministry posts rates of zakat assistance under various programs. Students in such programs receive varying amounts of zakat, with madrassah students receiving larger stipends in many cases. Because madrassah students typically do not pay for tuition and lodging and students in the mainstream sector do, the actual value of these stipends is even greater for madrassah students. In some cases madrassah students do not even pay for books and stationery. Thus in real terms, zakat allowances for students in religious educational programs are quite generous and provide a financial incentive for students to pursue religious studies.[74]

Preferences in the Educational Market

Interviews in Pakistan suggest a distinct status hierarchy of schools. English education is the most prized in terms of social status and employability.[75] Many employment advertisements explicitly request applicants who speak English, and parents naturally believe that English-language education imparts a skill that appears highly valued in the labor market. (An important empirical question is the extent to which such graduates acquire strong English skills at these schools.) Most persons interviewed noted that throughout most of the country's history, Pakistanis have not valued Islamic education per se. They have historically looked down upon the imam and conferred little social status on him, at least partly because his earnings were meager and depended on the largesse of the community he served.

However, many families hope that their children will learn to read the Quran and in many cases that at least one child will even attain the prized status of hafez. Pakistanis, like Muslims elsewhere, believe that when one becomes a hafez, spiritual advantages accrue not only to the individual but also to the family. Thus by requiring their child to become a hafez, parents are investing not only in the spiritual and social capital of the individual child, but also in the spiritual and social capital of the immediate and extended family. Irrespective of past views of religious education, many interlocutors interviewed for this study observed that over the past decade or so, Pakistanis have increasingly valued Islamic education.

When queried about the reasons for the increased esteem allegedly accorded Islamic education, some interviewees said this trend is related to international pressure on the government to deal harshly with its madaris in the wake of the September 11 terrorist attacks. They characterized this revitalized reverence as a kind of nationalistic response in defense of an institution seen as Pakistani and integral to Pakistan's identity as a Muslim state. Others, particularly madrassah administrators, believed that parents trusted madaris and the quality of the education they impart. Other interlocutors believed this purported trend was because the public education system was so problematic, teaching a 100-year-old curriculum using colonial-era methods promulgated by Thomas B. Macaulay in the nineteenth century.[76]

The research by Andrabi et al. may support the notion that families do seem to want at least one child to pursue religious education. Among families using madaris, only 23.5 percent enrolled their children exclusively in madaris. The majority of madrassah households (nearly 50 percent) use both madaris and public schools to educate their children, and another 28 percent use madaris and private schools *or all three school types simultaneously.*[77]

Recent work by Mathew Nelson also supports the idea that families in Pakistan value religious education as a fundamental feature of a good education. In summer 2003 Nelson interviewed 112 parents of school-age children in Rawalpindi, a large Punjabi city about ten miles south of Pakistan's capital, Islamabad. That team selected their sample to ensure that families had madrassah as well as non-madrassah options. In other words, they chose localities where a madrassah was one of at least two schooling options (in addition to public or private school). His team also interviewed leaders of several non-governmental organizations (NGOs) and personnel from donor organizations such the United Nations Children's Education Fund (UNICEF) and the United States Agency for International Development (USAID).

Among other survey questions, the Nelson team asked parents to identify first and secondary choices out of five specified educational priorities: basic education, religious education, liberal education, vocational education, and civic education. Respondents could also elect "other" to indicate preferences not stated in the survey. It is important to recall that religious education is not the exclusive purview of the madaris and is available in public and some private schools. Thus Nelson asked about priorities, not school type.

Overall, 41 percent of parents identified religious education as their primary priority and another 26 percent identified it as their second priority. In contrast, donors assumed that parents would turn away from religious education toward vocational education, illuminating the disconnection between parent preferences and what donors and NGOs believe about parents' preferences.[78]

Nelson's team did find variation in parental preferences when they disaggregated the data according to the level of respondents' educational attainment. Parents with no education overwhelmingly identified religious education as their first priority (71 percent). A majority of parents with a religious educational background (67 percent) also prioritized religious education. Well-educated parents (with a B.A., M.A., or Ph.D.) were more evenly distributed in their preferences for all options except vocational education, which garnered a mere 5 percent. Among well-educated Pakistanis, 21 percent identified basic education as their primary objective; 26 percent chose civic education; 21 percent selected liberal education; and 18 percent chose religious education. Thus although well-educated parents were less likely to identify religious education as their primary objective, nearly one in five did prioritize religious education over other types.[79]

A perusal of the educational market in Pakistan also confirms this preference for Islamic education. As noted elsewhere, numerous new schools combine mainstream education with Islamic education. In many cases these schools are so new that they have not produced a graduating class, or very few batches that can be evaluated for quality using national exam scores. For example, the new school Darul Uloom Islamiya in Islamabad has had only two graduating batches.[80] However, schools visited during fieldwork that have had batches were quick to point out when their students excelled in exams and won medals for their high marks. Although the Iqra school I visited in Lahore had yet to produce a medal winner in the exams, all their students had passed the Lahore board exams. The administrator interviewed noted that Iqra in Karachi (where the movement began) had produced a number of students who tested with distinction. However, aside from interviews with administrators eager to prove the quality of their students, others yielded little indication that this status hierarchy relies on objective performance measures of school quality. Presumably parents might care more about such measures, as they are in principle available.

Although madrassah administrators are quick to defend their institutions, many madaris are bringing new non-Islamic educational products to the market. In some cases madaris are opening English-language schools; in other cases they are opening Urdu-medium schools using the government-prescribed curriculum. These programs vary considerably. Some teach Islamic studies, while other madrassah-run schools—astonishingly—do not. These madrassah-run mainstream schools also vary in their fee structures. Some are heavily subsidized for poorer students, but other schools charge rates comparable to those of Pakistan's elite private schools. Parents are willing to pay these fees, and administrators claim that they receive more applications than they can admit.

The madaris are leveraging the reputation for quality they have developed as well as the trust they enjoy among parents to provide a nonreligious product. Parents feel reassured that their children are obtaining a high-quality mainstream education in an Islamic environment—even when Islamic subjects are not explicitly included in the curriculum. Apart from these madrassah business ventures in mainstream education, new schools seeking to combine elements of both continue to come into the market, and parents seem willing to pay high fees for these programs.

Although these market observations confirm the views expressed by interviewees, survey data I analyzed also suggest that in 2002, 70 percent of interviewed Pakistanis indicated they strongly supported madrassah reform; another 20 percent somewhat supported reform.[81] (See figure 1.) It is unfortunate that these data are available only for one year and that the question as asked gives little insight as to what is meant by madrassah reform.

More generally, Islamist institutions and leaders continue to enjoy support among Pakistanis, notwithstanding their approval of some kind of unspecified madrassah reform and even though large numbers of surveyed Pakistanis are less forthcoming in their support. For instance, the same survey found that 57 percent of respondents indicated they had a great deal or a fair amount of confidence in Pakistan's religious leaders. But 38 percent of respondents indicated having either not very

Figure 1. Do You Support or Oppose Madrassah Reform? Strongly or Somewhat?

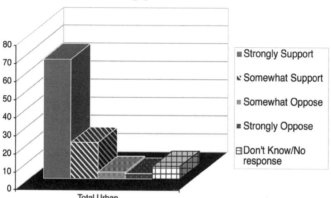

Source: Fair, "The Practice of Islam In Pakistan," 75–108.

much or no confidence in them. (Only 5 percent did not answer the question.)[82]

Data collected by Pew in 2002 and 2005 demonstrate a similar ambivalence in Pakistani opinion toward the role of Islam in public life. Pew asked respondents about the role they perceived Islam to be playing and the role it should play in public life. Although a majority believed that Islam was playing a very large role (75 percent), only 35 percent believed that it should play a very large role. Another 21 percent said it should play a fairly large role, compared to 11 percent who said it was playing a fairly large role. Combined, 27 percent believed Islam should play either a fairly small role or a very small role, compared to only 3 percent who said Islam was playing either a fairly small or a very small role. (Seventeen percent of those surveyed did not answer the question.) For 2002, it appears, a large swath of respondents appeared to believe that Islam had influence in Pakistan's political life to an inappropriate degree.[83]

In 2005 Pew changed the way it probed this issue. Surveyors first asked respondents whether Islam was playing a greater or lesser role in the country's politics. They then asked respondents whether this was good or bad for the country. In spring 2005, 48 percent of respondents indicated Islam was playing a greater role. Of this 48 percent, 94 percent believed this trend was good for the country. A minority, 23 percent, believed that Islam was playing a lesser role; of these only 24 percent believed this was good for the country. The largest fraction, 69 percent, indicated this was bad for the country.[84] Taken together, these data confirm that although important and large segments of Pakistanis affirm and support the importance of Islam in the country's political life, many do not welcome this role.

Conclusion

Islamic education in Pakistan is not the concern only of the madaris. In fact Islamic Studies is a compulsory subject in Pakistan's public schools, the sector that educates more than 70 percent of enrolled students. Formal religious education is the focus of the madrassah, which, in contrast, educates on average less than 1 percent of Pakistan's full-time students. Although a larger fraction of poor students attend madaris than either private or public schools, 12 percent of madrassah students come from Pakistan's wealthiest families; nearly a third are from families that are well-off by Pakistani standards.

Contrary to popular belief, madaris are not the school of last resort. In fact, where no non-madrassah alternatives exist, families simply exit the system, although weak evidence shows that madrassah attendance is more intense among poorer households than richer households, controlling for other factors. These trends hold even though Pakistan's system of zakat gives preference to Islamic schools through larger net subsidies for such education.

Taken together, various studies of madrassah and other school attendance strongly suggest that many families choose to send their children for specific functional reasons rather than their inability to afford other options or the lack of other alternatives. The fact that there is more variation within families than among families also supports this claim. Recall that most madrassah households used public or private schools for at least one child. The notion that parents choose religious education is buttressed by an examination of the educational market, which has been quick to present elite families with new options for combining religious and worldly education.

If religious educational preferences are not rooted in poverty or access and reflect an explicit preference by the family, perhaps little can be done in the short term to shift parental choice away from madaris for families that choose to use them. Large proportions of Pakistanis do reaffirm that they believe Islam is playing a greater role in the country and overall this is good for Pakistan—even though important sectors do not welcome this development. That said, at least one data point suggests some degree of support for madrassah reform.

Given that family choice of religious education may have little elasticity of demand and that overall madaris have a small and historically stable or declining market share, Pakistani and foreign policymakers should prioritize expanding access to public and possibly private-school enrollment. This in turn implies making a commitment to expanding the supply of schools with quality teachers of appropriate gender. However, as the foregoing discussion implies, parents may opt out of the market if perceived return on the educational investment seems inadequate. This return on investment may have as much to do with returns on education in the labor market as with the attributes of a particular school. Thus government-affected supply-side interventions to expand schools and teachers are unlikely to see expected return unless the determinants of parental choice are clearly understood and incorporated into these government reform ventures. As public schools educate 70 percent of Pakistan's students and private schools 30 percent, effort should be made to focus on curriculum reform as appropriate and required. Based on an analysis of the overall educational market, the policy focus on madaris seems misplaced. Other factors, such as ties to madaris and militancy, which may require attention to madaris for non-educational reasons, must also be considered.

2

A Deeper Look at Pakistan's Islamic Schools

R eligious education takes place in Pakistan at both formal and informal religious educational institutions. Formal primary education takes place in makatib, and secondary and postsecondary Islamic education takes place in madaris. In addition, graduates of the madaris with Alimiyah degrees can specialize in post-Alimiyah subjects (Hadith, *iftah*, and others) at specialized madaris or the International Islamic University; or they can go to Islamic universities abroad. Islamic education also happens in the public sector through Islamiyat in the government-prescribed curriculum. In addition, new kinds of educational programs such as the Iqra schools, which combine worldly and religious education, have come onto the market. Other chains that impart Islamic education to a wider audience and in settings that differ from the traditional madrassah include Al Huda and Tameer-i-Millat, among others.[1]

Apart from these formal programs of studies, numerous informal opportunities exist to learn more about Islam. These aim to enable men and women, as well as young adults, to acquire a deeper understanding of their faith while not enrolled in a formal institution of learning. For example, Dars-e-Quran, are conducted in people's homes. Members of the Tablighi Jamaat, a Deobandi-influenced organization dedicated to the propagation of Islam, are also required to go on *daura*, a circuit of propagation. However, little systematic information is available about these informal opportunities, which students enrolled in mainstream institutions or adults not in the educational system may attend. In other words, informal education may not be a "substitute good" for formal education but, rather, a "complementary good." Other programs (such as Tablighi Jamaat and Al Huda) aim to impart greater Islamic knowledge to adults and may complement formal education in many cases. Here I focus on the formal Islamic education provided at madaris because it is this system that produces ulama and religious studies teachers.

Table 6. Expansion of Deeni Madaris between 1947 and 2000 by Region

Province/Area	1947	1960	1980	1988	2000
Punjab	121	195	1,012	1,320	3,153
Sarhad (NWFP)	59	87	426	678	1,281
Sindh	21	87	380	291	905
Baluchistan	28	70	135	347	692
Azad Kashmir	4	8	29	76	151
Islamabad	--	1	27	47	94
Northern Areas	12	16	47	102	185
FATA	--	--	--	--	300
Total	245	464	2056	2861	6,741

Source: Ministry of Religious Affairs, *1979 Report;* Ministry of Education, 1988, 2000. Compiled in Khalid, *Deeni Madaris main taleem, 145.*

How Many Madaris?

One of the most vexing questions posed by policymakers concerns the numbers of religious schools in Pakistan. Estimates in the popular literature have ranged from 5,000 to 45,000.[2] These estimates have been problematic because they rely heavily on interview data and because of the pervasive confusion between madaris and makatib. The popular accounts generally have overlooked government surveys of madaris (distinct from makatib), including a report from 1979 by the Ministry of Religious Affairs and two reports by the Ministry of Education in 1989 and 2000. These reports suggest that as of 2000, there were 6,741 registered madaris in Pakistan. Table 6 provides a historical count of madaris, using these government data sources.

It may be desirable to count the madaris in Pakistan, but this may be nearly impossible for at least three reasons. Aside from the definitional problem, there is no central database of registered madaris at present. Registration happens at the district level, and those documents are all in hard copies filed with local governments. Second, it is highly likely that the records are woefully out of date. Touquir Shah, a former government official charged with madrassah registration among other duties, found that once madaris file their registration, they rarely update those records—even if the madrassah has changed location.[3] Third, records are only for registered madaris.

An Overview of Formal Islamic Schools

Although madaris and makatib have a number of apparent similarities, they differ fundamentally in the scope of their curricula and their primary operational objectives.[4] The sina qua non of madaris is the Dars-i-Nizami, or Alim course, which must be mastered before one becomes an alim. The curriculum was devised by Mulla Nizamuddin Sihalvi (died 1748), a scholar in Islamic jurisprudence and philosophy at Farangi Mahal, a famous madrassah in Lucknow.[5] This is not the same curriculum propounded by Mullah Nasiruddin Tusi (died 1064) at the Madrassah Nizamia he established in eleventh-century Baghdad.[6] Almost all Sunni madaris—irrespective of whether their sectarian affiliation is Barelvi, Ahl-e-Hadith, Jamaat-i-Islami, or Deobandi—follow this course of study, which was formally adopted by the Deoband seminary (in India) in 1867. Each interpretative school naturally modifies the curriculum according to its sectarian requirements. This is so because imparting a particular sectarian worldview and defending it against the teachings of other interpretative schools are critical to the educational mission of creating scholars in each sectarian tradition.[7] The Shia madaris have a similar multiyear curriculum. (See table 7.)

The Alim course is generally an eight-year course of study in Sunni madaris if students come into the system with an eighth- or tenth-grade qualification. In addition, there is a condensed six-year program for female students to accommodate early marriage.[8] Some madaris have

Table 7. Programs of Madrassah Study and Their Chronological Equivalency to Nonreligious School

Level (Darja)	Level	Class	Duration	Certificate (Sanad)	Comparable to Mainstream Education
Ibtidaya	Nazara	1–5	4–5 yrs	Shahadatul Tahfeez ul Quran	Primary (5th grade)
Mutawassitah	Hifz	6–8	3 yrs	Shahadatul Mutawassitah	Middle (8th)
Thanviyah -e- Ammah	Tajveed, Qeeraat	Ulla va Thanviyah (9, 10)	2 yrs	Shahadatul Thanviyah ul Amma	Matric (10th)
Thanviyah-e-Kassah	Tehtani (Higher secondary)	Arbiat va Ashara (11–12)	2 yrs	Shahadatul Thanviyah-e-Kassah	Intermediate (F.A.)
Aliya	Mohqufaleh Khasa va Sada (College)	Arbiat va Ashara (13,14)	2 yrs	Shahadatul Aliya	B.A.
Alimiyah	Daura Hadiths Sabia va Saniya	Master phil Arabia phil Uluum al Islamia (15–16)	2 yrs	Shahadatul Alimiyah phil Uluum Arabia vul Islamia	M.A. recognized as such. in Arabic and Islamic studies by government
Takmeel	Post-graduate	Varies with specialization	1 yr	Varies with specialization	Post-M.A.

Source: Khalid, *Deeni Madaris main taaleem,* 144.

programs that take many more years to finish, depending on how they expand the Alim course and how they have integrated it with new worldly subjects. For example, Jamia Binoria (SITE) has a sixteen-year program that combines religious and worldly education from the first-grade. Darul Uloom Islamiya's program is eleven years long and begins only after the students complete Hifz-e-Quran, which usually takes two to three years. By the time students finish their course of study, they have completed the highest degree offered in the madrassah system (Alimiyah) as well as their B.A. from Punjab University. (Their students appear as private candidates for the Punjab University exams.)

At Kher ul Madaris the length of study is seventeen years, and it begins after the fifth grade—not the tenth grade. For hafez this condition is waived. The Mutawassitah program is a year long and covers the subjects usually covered in grades six, seven, and eight. Their Thanvi-yah-e-Ammah is a three-year program that covers the standard Dars-i-Nizami subjects for that level, as well as the worldly subjects for grades nine and ten. The Sanviyaa Khasa level comprises two years and covers Dars-i-Nizami subjects, as well as grades eleven and twelve. Aliya takes two years, covering religious subjects and worldly subjects in grades thirteen and fourteen. Alimiyah is two years long and covers religious subjects along with those of grades fifteen and sixteen.

The Alim course and Dars-i-Nizami curriculum cover a total of some twenty subjects that fall into two categories: *al-uloom al-naqliya* (transmitted sciences) and *al-uloom al-aqliya* (rational sciences). Of these twenty subjects, only about half can be called religious per se or directly relevant to the production of religious scholars. These include dialectical theology, life of the Prophet, Hadith, *tafseer* (exegesis of the Quran), Islamic law, jurisprudence, rhetoric, and grammar, as well as Arabic literature and logic. Other subjects (medicine, mathematics, astronomy, history, philosophy, prosody, and polemics) were included in this nineteenth-century curriculum to equip students for civil service jobs and help them understand religious texts.[9] A sample reading list for Arabic texts used in a typical Deobandi Dars-i-Nizami is in appendix B. The date of publication is not available for all of these texts, but the years in which the authors died are. As data in appendix B demonstrate, the authors of these standard texts lived in the eighth through twentieth centuries, with a heavy concentration of authors from the thirteenth through the fifteenth centuries.[10]

One should not conclude that because these "rational sciences" are included in the curriculum, students are receiving a well-rounded education. First, not all madaris teach all of these subjects anymore. Second, for those that do retain them, the texts are all classical, as appendix B shows. The texts used for philosophy and logic date back to the thirteenth through the nineteenth centuries. The medical textbooks are from the eleventh, thirteenth, and fifteenth centuries. Seena's eleventh-century text is still considered to be a legitimate study of pathology and anatomy despite the fact that this book is eleven centuries out of date. The books used to teach astronomy and mathematics are all 300 to 700 years old.[11]

In addition to the Alim course, some madaris have specialized faculty for subjects such as tafseer, hadith, iftah, or fiqh. These high-level programs are only for students who have completed Dars-i-Nizami and may take at least two years to complete, depending on the subject and the desired level of qualification.

Madrassah administrators claim that the terminal sanad (Alimiyah) offered through Dars-i-Nizami is recognized by the government as equivalent to an M.A. in Arabic and Islamic studies. For most purposes this is not strictly true, as will be shown below. Although President Zulfiqar Ali Bhutto first proposed equating these degrees to appease and co-opt Islamists challenging his government, it was President and General Zia ul Haq who formally extended equivalencies of the Alimiyah to the M.A. degree. The terms of this equivalency have been and remain disputed and subject to poorly understood caveats, which the government of Pakistan has used in recent years to exert control over the pool of persons contesting elections.

Such manipulation was apparent in the 2002 general elections, when the Pakistan Election Commission declared that candidates standing for election to public office must have at least a B.A. qualification and determined that the Alimiyah sanad would be accepted as an equivalent to an M.A. To extend this equivalency, the government waived the usual preconditions for comparability established by the University Grants Commission, which requires that B.A. candidates successfully pass exams in English, Urdu, and Pakistan studies. This set of rulings disqualified most of the candidates from the mainstream parties because most people in Pakistan do not reach the postsecondary level. However, candidates from the religious parties were permitted to contest elections because many of them were ulama with the highest madrassah degree. This ruling ensured the modest political successes of Islamist parties in that election.[12]

Since 2002 many Islamists elected to office have proved to be a nuisance to the government. To press-gang obstreperous Islamist politicians into cooperating with the government, the Musharraf government pressured the Supreme Court to disqualify their candidacies on the grounds of inadequate educational attainment. With the removal from office of vocal Islamist opponents, the threat of disqualification loomed over other Islamist politicians who possessed only madrassah degrees. Reflecting the growing challenge that Islamist candidates posed to the Musharraf government, it reversed the equivalency of degrees for the 2005 local body elections. Alimiyah holders were not allowed to run—even if they had in 2002—without also holding a bachelor's degree or having passed the additional exams noted above.[13]

Despite the madrassah officials' contention that their terminal degrees are widely accepted as M.A. equivalents, this is still a hotly contested issue with no resolution in sight. It continues to give the Musharraf government considerable space to manipulate the field of potential electoral candidates and the behavior of serving and aspiring Islamist politicians. It was not clear at the time of writing how this issue would be dealt with in the elections scheduled for fall 2007 or early 2008.

Although no statistics exist on this issue, many people I interviewed contended that most madaris in Pakistani do not offer the terminal sanad (Alimiyah). Instead, they offer educational programs up to one of the three sanads below Alimiyah, including Aliya, Thanviyah Khasa, and Thanviya Amma. Consequently students may complete part of their studies at a local madrassah but must transfer to a larger madrassah to finish the Alimiyah degree. For this reason madrassah administrators are loath to discuss "dropouts" because they claim that students are not leaving religious studies; rather, they are moving on to complete higher levels of study. They claim to have no ability to track students who leave studies or continue at another madrassah.

Unlike the Alimiyah, these lower certificates have no formal equivalency to degrees offered by the various Pakistan government educational boards. The schedule for the various degrees and their rough chronological equivalent in the worldly educational sector are in table 7. It should be noted that madrassah students can prepare in many cases for the government curriculum exams and take exams alongside public school students for their matriculation, fine arts, and bachelor's degrees.

Madrassah Organization

The vast majority of madaris in Pakistan are associated with one of five *wafaq* (roughly translated as educational boards). Each wafaq represents one of five *masalik* (literally, ways or paths; singular *maslak*). This term designates the particular interpretative tradition and sectarian affiliation of the board. Four of the boards are Sunni (Deobandi, Ahl-e-Hadith, Barelvi, and Jamaat-i-Islami) and one is Shia.[14] The full name of each wafaq, its date of founding, and the central location of its board (*markaz*) are in table 8.

Madaris associated with these five boards teach according to the Dars-i-Nizami curriculum; however, they may use different texts. The specific texts used by the five boards reflect their theological viewpoint (madhab or maslak) and serve to clarify and motivate theological points of difference between Sunni and Shia or within Sunni traditions (Deobandi, Ahl-e-Hadith, Barelvi). An important component of madrassah education is refutation (*radd*), by which students learn to counter the theological worldviews of other maslaks, heretical beliefs, and some Western concepts. Students are also taught to marshal arguments in defense of their maslak.[15] As will be discussed later, this has led several scholars to suggest a link between madrassah education and sectarian conflict in Pakistan.[16] Although it is beyond the scope of this volume to delineate in great detail the theological differences among these schools, a few comments about each are in order.

Deobandis

The Deoband tradition in what is now Pakistan began with Maulana Muhammad Qasim Nanautawi (1833–1877) and Maulana Rashid

Ahmed Gangohi (1829–1905), who founded the famous madrassah Darul Uloom at Deoband (in the present-day Indian state of Uttar Pradesh) in 1867. Deoband departed from the traditional madrassah structure in South Asia in that it had a regular organizational framework, including a rector, a chancellor, and a chief instructor. Its curriculum was based on the Dars-i-Nizami curriculum. The Deoband was a reformist movement that sought to purify Islam of syncretic components in mystical orders associated with saints and prophets, which were seen as deriving from the Hindu practices of the subcontinent.[17] Since Pakistan's independence in 1947 Deobandis have become more strident in opposing mystical practices.

Significantly, one of two most important Islamist political parties, JUI, is a Deobandi organization, with high-level political leaders receiving their education from Deobandi madaris. Many JUI politicians are Deoband-trained ulama. Currently two factions (JUI-Fazlur Rehman and JUI-Sami ul Haq) are part of the six-member coalition of Islamist parties that comprise the "loyal opposition," the Muttahida Majlis-e-Amal (MMA). The MMA has forty-five seats in the 272-member National Assembly and is the ruling party in the NWFP. It rules in coalition with President Musharraf's party, the Pakistan Muslim League-Qaid (PML-Q) in Baluchistan.[18]

In the 1990s several JUI/Deobandi madaris became notorious for educating Taliban leaders and supporting the Taliban in Afghanistan politically, financially, and even militarily. Maulana Sami ul Haq, who heads an important faction of JUI, ran one of the most important madaris in Akora Khatak. It helped train the Taliban, provided personnel to their effort to take over Afghanistan in the 1990s, and even helped them fight U.S. forces during the ongoing U.S. military operation in Afghanistan Operation Enduring Freedom (October 2007–present). More problematic is the fact that Deobandi madaris and ulama have been associated with a number of militant Pakistani groups that claim to fight in Afghanistan and Kashmir (Harkat ul Jihad, Jaish-e-Mohamad, Harkat ul Ansar), as well as anti-Shia sectarian groups (Lashkar-e-Jhangvi and Sipah-e-Sahaba-e-Pakistan) and a number of organizations (Jundullah, among others) that have begun targeting the state itself in recent years.[19]

Table 8. Five Wafaq-al Madaris

Name of Wafaq	Maslak (Sect or Sub-Sect)	Date Founded	Location of Markaz
Wafaq-ul-Madaris-al-Arabia Pakistan (Deobandi)	Sunni-Hanafi-Deobandi (known as Deobandi)	1959	Multan
Tanzeem-ul-Madaris (Barelvi)	Sunni-Hanafi-Barelvi (known as Barelvi)	1960	Lahore
Wafaq-ul-Madaris-al-Salafia (Ahl-e-Hadith)	Sunni-Ahle-e-Hadiths (known as Salafi)	1955	Faisalabad
Rabitatul Madaris Al Islamiya (Jamaat-i-Islami)	Jamaat-i-Islami	1983	Mansoora (Lahore)
Wafaq-ul-Madaris-Shia (Shia)	Shia	1959	Lahore

Source: Khalid, *Deeni Madaaris Main Taleem*, 143.

Barelvis

The Barelvi movement traces its origins to Ahmed Raza Khan of Barelvi (1856–1921). Pakistanis have been traditional adherents of this movement, which is often called "folk Islam" or "Sufi Islam." Barelvis embrace heterodox practices and beliefs such as devotion to shrines, celebration of auspicious dates, and veneration of graves. They also believe that *pirs* (heads of Sufi orders) can intercede with God on behalf of their followers and disciples. Both the Deobandi and the Ahl-e-Hadith ulama vehemently reject these heterodox beliefs and practices.[20]

Ahl-e-Hadith

This interpretative tradition began in nineteenth-century Bhopal (now in India), drawing on the ideas of two Indian religious scholars, Sayyid Ahmad Brelwi (died 1831) and Waliullah Dihlawi (died 1763), as well as a Yemeni scholar, Muhammad b'Ali ash-Shaukani (died 1832). Although claiming to follow no particular school of Islamic jurisprudence, this tradition emerged as an Islamic reform movement that challenged religious practices it saw as "unlawful innovations." Ahl-e-Hadith teachings are similar to those of the Saudi Arabian Wahhabi movement. Because the term Wahhabi has pejorative connotations, Ahl-e-Hadith proponents reject that label. Ahl-e-Hadith madaris also teach the Dars-i-Nizami curriculum, but they emphasize the Quran and the Hadith and ardently oppose folk traditions that Barelvis practice, such as death anniversaries of pirs, mystical beliefs, and distribution of food on religious occasions.[21] The Ahl-e-Hadith maslak also has political representation, including one party (Markazi Jamiat Al-Hadith-Sajid Mir) that is part of the MMA.

Jamaat-i-Islami

This religious political party was founded in 1941 by Abul ala Maududi (died 1979), who is still Pakistan's most influential Islamist thinker. The Jamaat-i-Islami persists as the most ideologically coherent of Pakistan's political parties.[22] Maududi himself was very much influenced by the Deobandis and Tablighi Jama'at and was deeply and adversely affected by Hindu nationalists' activities, including "reconversion" of Muslims. Maududi's ideology mixed "Muslimness" with pressing issues of nationhood, separatism, sovereignty, and territorial borders. Although Maududi's ideology was nationalist in motivation, it was universalistic in outlook. This universalism quickly became part of Jamaat-i-Islami's mission, which includes shunning sectarian divisions in the *umma*.[23]

Jamaat-i-Islami branches also exist in India, Kashmir, Bangladesh, and Sri Lanka. The varied branches in these states have relations with one another but operate independently. Since Pakistan's independence Jamaat-i-Islami has become trusted by the state and increasingly assumed a role in the formulation and prosecution of its domestic and foreign policies. Jamaat-i-Islami madaris use the Dars-i-Nizami curriculum, although they also emphasize politics, economics, and history, in keeping with their goal of producing ulama who can confront Western ideas.[24]

Since Pakistan's independence Jamaat-i-Islami has been in direct command and control of several militant groups (such as Hizbol Mujahadeen and Al Badr) that operate primarily in Indian-administered Kashmir. With ideological affinity to the Egyptian Muslim Brotherhood and the notoriety of having harbored several al Qaeda activists, Jamaat-i-Islami is believed to be closer to al Qaeda than the Deobandis, who came into contact with al Qaeda principally through the Taliban.[25] Along with JUI, Jamaat-i-Islami is one the two most important parties in the MMA.

Shia

In addition to the four Sunni boards, Pakistan also has Shia madaris. Shia believe that the Prophet's rightful successor was Ali Abn-e-Abi Talib and therefore reject the tenure of the first three caliphs, whom Sunnis accept as the Prophet's successors. Shia madaris in Pakistan use the Dars-i-Nizami curriculum with different texts.[26] In the past, there were also several notorious Shia militant groups; however, these have been largely eliminated by the government and through anti-Shia militias. Shia political parties remain but are very weak. One of these, Islami Tehreek-e-Pakistan, is a member of the MMA.

Madrassah Faculty

Because comprehensive data on madrassah faculty are scant, I rely on interview data to make a number of observations here. Madrassah administrators were asked about their criteria for hiring. At the formal madaris, the foremost requirement was that the potential instructor had completed the Alim course (had his Alim sanad) from a board associated with the madrassah in question. In other words, a graduate from a Deobandi madrassah would not be employed at an Ahl-e-Hadiths madrassah. Sometimes the teacher must be a hafez or a qari, but not always. Jami'a Muntazir, a Shia madrassah, departs from this general rule. For teachers at the lower levels of the Alim curriculum (Kamrul Fazal), the teacher need only be qualified for Alimiya; a sanad is not required. However, for higher levels (Sultan ul Fazal and Alimiya), the teacher must be qualified for Alimiya and have the sanad and a qualification from Najaf or Qom. Rarely did any administrator mention the desire to have Ph.D.-qualified teachers; in fact most observers of religious education in Pakistan believe that it is not desirable to hire a teacher with a Ph.D.[27]

The madaris I visited varied in their required level of teaching experience. For example, in some cases madaris would permit their own higher-class students to teach students on the lower levels of the curriculum. Some madaris explicitly prefer to hire their own students. At Kher ul Madaris, they prefer to hire their own graduates and assign levels of courses to be taught based on an evaluation of the former student's performance at the madrassah. For outside hires Kher ul Madaris imposes a minimum of five years' experience. Generally speaking, senior teachers are assigned the higher levels of instruction, while junior teachers are assigned the lower levels. For example, at Dar ul Uloom Sarhad, teachers hired at the Alimiya level have to have good marks and a long record of teaching. (Their most experienced teacher has twenty years' experience.) For lower level courses, they require less experience.

Among the madaris I visited, variable standards were imposed for language ability as a precondition of hiring. At Dar ul Uloom Sarhad teachers do not need to speak Arabic or Persian, but they must know and be able to teach the books used at the madrassah, most of which are in Arabic and some of which are in Persian. At all madaris visited during fieldwork, the language of instruction is generally Urdu, with a few madaris and teachers using Arabic. At Jamia Banuria, English and Arabic are used exclusively in its foreign student section.

At most schools I visited, administrators explained that there was no "job talk," where the candidate would be compelled to demonstrate his ability to teach. Most noted that the candidate would be interviewed and this would provide an opportunity to assess the academic life and intellectual capabilities of the candidate. Administrators noted that they often hired their own graduates, which gave them the opportunity to hire known quantities, as many of these graduates would have taught at lower levels of the Alim course.

At Darul Uloom Islamiya in Islamabad they need teachers who can teach worldly subjects. For these positions Alim qualification is not needed if the teacher is qualified in a secular subject. However, the candidate must "have proper Islamic dress" or be willing to adopt such dress. (This means a beard of appropriate length, shalwar kameez, a cap, and so forth.) For some subjects, such as English language, they would even consider hiring someone not of their maslak if necessary. Iqra has a similar problem in its need for teachers with worldly qualifications who are willing to wear Islamic dress. For the worldly education program Iqra requires that teachers have at least a B.A. A B.Ed. is not required, and many of their teachers of worldly subjects actually have

M.A. and M.Sc. qualifications. For teachers in the worldly education section, an Islamic education is not required.

Administrators and teachers at the various madaris I visited differed in preference for and availability of foreign qualified teachers. Almost all interlocutors claimed to prize foreign qualifications, but even the prestigious madaris had very few foreign-qualified and even fewer foreign teachers. They claimed that this was because of a number of problems with hiring foreigners. For instance, at Jamia Ashrafia administrators said that foreign qualification was highly desirable and they would like to have teachers from the United States, Saudi Arabia, and Al Azhar. The problem is that they cannot afford to meet high expectations of salary and expatriate standards of living. (Jamia Ashrafiya's average income of Rs.10,000–12,000 ($166–199) per month, with free accommodation on the premises, is not desirable to expatriates or foreign-qualified nationals.) At Jamia Muntazir foreign qualification is required for higher-level teaching. In fact they make special efforts to hire such teachers, and they lower their experience threshold for them.

Administrators generally claimed to have no information about the social background of their teachers or even about their political affiliation or roles in political parties. This seemed difficult to believe in many cases. For example, many of the Deobandi administrators I interviewed were also deeply involved in the Deobandi Islamist political party JUI. Moreover, many of my meetings were cancelled or rescheduled to permit faculty and student participation in the political rallies responding to publication of Danish cartoons of the Prophet in February 2006. Press accounts featuring the statements of these persons were published in the newspapers the next day. When confronted with this fact, most administrators claimed that the rallies were not about politics. In my view this statement was largely disingenuous, given that the rallies were almost exclusively about politics and provided ample opportunity to attack the Musharraf government as well as the United States, which had little or nothing to do with the cartoons.

Madrassah Students

As noted elsewhere, survey data suggest that lower- and lower-middle-class children are more likely to attend a madrassah than their wealthier counterparts. Similarly, children in rural areas are more likely to attend madaris. Household surveys discussed above also note that the highest madrassah enrollment tends to be along the Pakistan-Afghanistan border. But the data also show that many students from wealthier strata and urban areas do attend madaris.

These household survey data are consistent with data obtained during interviews with madrassah administrators and teachers. Although these interlocutors conceded that many students came from rural, lower-, and lower-middle-class backgrounds, almost every madrassah administrator noted that 10 to 30 percent came from higher socioeconomic strata. Administrators from programs that include girls' education noted that female students overwhelmingly came from the wealthier sectors of Pakistani society. At schools I visited, administrators said girls' families paid fees to the madrassah for their education. They explained that girls do not become ulama, and families value this education because madrassah-educated girls obtain better marital alliances than girls who are not madrassah-trained. Madrassah education is likely to be associated with the girl's decency (and by extension the family's decency) and the likelihood that she will raise observant and honorable children.

Administrators at most of the elite madaris I visited claimed that students must have at least an eighth-grade qualification for admission, with a preference for a tenth-grade qualification. If this standard is imposed with any rigor, it must be kept in mind that the schools visited for this study are the most prestigious madaris in Pakistan, and more than others they can impose such qualifications because demand for their seats always exceeds supply.[28] Analysts of madaris in Islamabad cautioned that very few madaris have these standards, and in their view the vast majority of madaris have no such standards.

During my visits to the various schools, visual inspection suggested that many children were too young to have met this criterion. This suggests that either exceptions must be frequent or the policy was promulgated quite recently. When questioned, most madrassah administrators conceded that this is a very new standard, except in Jamaat-i-Islami madaris that imposed it in the 1960s, and they do make exceptions. The novelty of this policy and the pervasiveness of exceptions was confirmed by Mahmood Ahmed Ghazi, a former cabinet member under Musharraf and president of the International Islamic University.

I asked madrassah administrators about other admission criteria for students. At Dar ul Uloom Sarhad the admission process is fairly minimal: The school does an interview with the student to assess his verbal skills and general behavior and to check to ensure that he is a matriculate. (They are flexible about the matriculation requirement when they feel it is appropriate.) At Jamia Tafeem ul Quran (JI), students must be matriculates and they must score at least 40 percent on an entrance exam administered by the madrassah. Kher ul Madaris also administers an exam to applicants who are entering from another madrassah. Exams are used to determine the level at which the student will begin studying at Kher ul Madaris. Such students must be matriculates and already have a religious education. Without it they start at the beginning of the madrassah's curriculum.

Some schools, such as Darul Uloom Islamiya, tend not to accept outsiders (give no lateral entry) into their program. Students can be accepted only at the beginning of the program. Presumably this is because it is so rigorous in its combination of worldly and religious education that few students who have come from either the worldly or religious educational stream could enter laterally. Some madaris require that all applicants be hafez. Jamia Muntazir requires that their students pass a medical exam to ensure they do not have communicable diseases. Some madaris (such as Muntazir) also inquire about the family to make sure it is honorable. Most madaris require that students be of the same maslak for various reasons. Madrassah administrators justified this restriction by noting that students outside their maslak do not apply to study there; differences between students and teachers would be disruptive and would undermine the ability of the madrassah to impart education as desired.

Most administrators claimed that their students did not participate in political activities, and most went further, saying that such participation is punishable. As noted, the timing of my visit to Pakistan in February 2006 corresponded with widespread agitation over the cartoon controversy. This gave me a good opportunity to assess the validity of that claim: Was the school open during the agitation or not? Schools like Jamia Banuria and Kher-ul-Madaris kept their appointments, and the school was open during the demonstrations. However, Banuri Town, Jamia Uloom Islamia, and Matla-ul-Uloom did not. At Banuri Town I observed that numerous advertisements for the protests had been posted in Urdu. (Presumably administrators had assumed that the advertisements and their significance would have gone unnoticed during my visits. They expressed discomfort when I asked about them.)

Conclusion

This chapter underscores the diversity and range of religious education in Pakistan, which takes place at both formal and informal religious educational institutions as well as public schools and spans primary, secondary, higher secondary, and postsecondary levels. It also shows the sectarian diversity of madaris within the five main sectarian divisions (maslaks) and, notably, their political affiliations and activities.

Unfortunately, popular accounts of madaris tend to depict them as expansive in number and engaging in little rigorous scholarly activity. However, a closer look at the madrassah curriculum undermines this characterization. Not only do these authors overestimate the number of madaris, they often do not appreciate that students who specialize in religious studies embark upon a complex and multilingual educational venture. However, even madrassah champions question the content and relevance of the archaic curriculum employed. Contemporary reports on Pakistan's madaris also tend to presume that Islamic education is the sole domain of religious institutions and overlook the other important venues of Islamic education.

Madaris also have political significance. As many of them have explicit ties with religious parties, they are important political actors despite their claims to the contrary. In fact, many madrassah officials are ranking members of the national or provincial chapters of the religious parties. Their students serve as an important source of street power that can be mobilized in the service of their political benefactors, as evidenced by the students' involvement in demonstrations and rallies. Ties between Islamist political actors, madaris, and student political activism are probably at the core of many of the policy debates surrounding madrassah reform. The political importance of madaris and ulama also conditions the government's decision about something as mundane as the madrassah degree (sanad) and eligibility of those who have such degrees to contest elections in Pakistan.

3

Madaris and Militancy

P erhaps one of the most pressing reasons for policymakers' attention to madaris is the putative link between these schools and militancy in Pakistan and beyond. The role of madaris in recruiting mujahideen during U.S. and international efforts to expel the Soviets from Afghanistan during the 1980s is well known. It is certain that some madaris along the Pakistan-Afghanistan border are linked to the ongoing militancy in North and South Waziristan and the insurgency in Afghanistan. No doubt, some madaris have ties to militant organizations and actively help channel potential recruits to their representatives.[1]

Reasons for Doubt: Views from the Supply Side of Militant Labor Supply

Notwithstanding these well-founded historical and current concerns, evidence counters the most sweeping contemporary claims that madaris are extensively involved in the production of militants in Pakistan and elsewhere. This evidence comes from studies of militants' characteristics. Such studies are often called "supply-side" because they enumerate the characteristics of militant manpower or labor supply. (The demanders of militant labor are the militant groups, or *tanzeems*, themselves.)

A number of scholarly supply-side studies include in-depth examination of the background of known militants. Mark Sageman, Alan Krueger, Peter Bergen, Claude Berrebi, and I collected extensive background information on Islamist militants and found that the vast majority of such persons were on average better educated (had higher educational attainment) than the populations from which they were recruited.[2] Krueger and Maleckova and Berrebi have studied suicide terrorists and found that generally *suicide* terrorists tend to have educational levels exceeding the societal mean and are less likely to live in poverty, relative to the average person. Their conclusions have echoed the recent findings of forensic psychiatrist Marc Sageman, who compiled profiles of 172 Salafist jihadists who have targeted foreign governments or people. In analyzing these collected profiles Sageman also contends that terrorists are less likely to be poor and undereducated than other individuals in the societies from which they are drawn. Peter Bergen also reviewed high-profile terrorists and found that they were not madrassah educated.[3]

However, none of these prominent studies have looked at Pakistan, where militants include military officers and enlisted personnel, well-educated operatives as well as madrassah graduates. In fact, unlike madaris in other locations, a limited number of madaris in Pakistan do produce suicide attackers who operate there as well as in Afghanistan. However, not all of Pakistan's suicide attackers come from madaris, as evidenced by the military personnel involved in various attempts to assassinate President Musharraf.[4] The military landscape is much more complex than is generally understood.

Evidence from a Survey of 141 Militant Families in Pakistan

To explore the connections between militancy and education, I commissioned a survey of families in Pakistan that had lost at least one son to militancy in Kashmir and Afghanistan in 2004. Pakistan-based researchers administered a comprehensive questionnaire to a convenience sample of 141 families mostly concentrated in the Punjab and North West Frontier Province. Families from Sindh, Baluchistan, and Pakistan-administered Kashmir were also included. The survey instrument collected limited personal information about the respondent (who in almost all cases was the male head of household); the household and its members; and, most important, the militant—including where he obtained militant training, where he served, and where he died; where and how he was recruited; his work and educational background; and his marital status at the time of recruitment and death.[5]

Of the 141 mujahideen in the data set, the vast majority served and died in Kashmir. Of these mujahideen, only nineteen were reportedly recruited at a madrassah—the same number recruited at a public school. Nobody was recruited at a private school. In contrast, according to respondents fifty militants were recruited through friends, thirty-two at mosques, twenty-seven through proselytizing groups (*tabligh*) and thirteen from relatives. (The numbers do not add up to 141 because some militants were recruited at multiple venues and some respondents did not answer the question.) Madaris are not the most prominent recruitment venue; indeed fewer than a quarter of the militants (33 of 141) ever attended madaris. Of those thirty-three madrassah products, twenty-seven attended a madrassah for four or fewer years, and most also attended public schools. In contrast, 82 of the 141 were very well educated by Pakistani standards, with at least a matriculation qualification (tenth-grade education), in stark contrast to the average level for Pakistani males (sixth grade). Only 9 of the 141 had no formal education. In the main, militants in this sample are much better educated than the average Pakistani male.[6]

These conclusions of supply-side studies found that in general militants are not undereducated or from madaris. At first blush these findings conflict with those of other prominent researchers, such as Collier and Hoeffler, who did find evidence, albeit not necessarily in Pakistan, that higher income and educational attainment should reduce the risk of political violence, principally by increasing the economic opportunity costs of participation in rebellion and other forms of violence.[7] These ostensible differences, between the work of Collier and Hoeffler on the one hand and the supply-side studies on the other, can be explained to a great extent by the recent work of Ethan Bueno de Mesquita.[8]

In Bueno de Mesquita's game-theory approach to understanding the interaction among a government, a terrorist organization, and potential terrorist volunteers, he finds that although individuals with low ability or little education are most likely to volunteer to join a terrorist organization, the organization screens the volunteers for quality. That is, terrorist groups, like other employers, impose standards of quality in their recruitment efforts and pick the most qualified person for the intended mission, subject to whatever resource constraints the organization faces.[9] Here "quality" refers to human capital endowment or simply aptitude. Thus "high quality" means a person above average in human capital endowment or aptitude; it is not a normative statement. Militant groups, like other employees, do not observe quality directly. Rather, they use market signals such as educational attainment, previous job experience, and recommendations of persons acquainted with the recruit to find the best match in skills for the desired operation.

Groups have the luxury of selecting the best recruit subject to their operational requirements as long as more persons are willing to join a group than the actual requirement for additional personnel. In other words, as long as militant recruitment is demand constrained, not supply constrained, groups can select the most qualified person for their mission. For some groups (such as the Taliban or sectarian militants) religious education may be an asset and confer some kinds of operational advantages to the organization. So in some cases persons with a religious educational background may be the preferred candidates. This is likely to be true for Taliban recruits (who historically are tied to Deobandi madaris in Pakistan) and for sectarian militants.

Available evidence suggests that madaris *are* important sources of supply of suicide attackers (in Afghanistan and Pakistan).[10] Attacks in Afghanistan are relevant because many—if not most—employ attackers from madaris in Pakistan's tribal area. The reasons for this are not quite clear. In the case of Afghanistan, the validity of suicide attacks as an acceptable means of warfare are contested, with many Afghans seeing them as suicide rather than a legitimate mode of waging jihad. In fact, in both Pakistan and Afghanistan, popular support for suicide attacks is relatively low, with 11 percent and 9 percent, respectively indicating that suicide attacks (even in defense of Islam) are always or sometimes justified.[11] In contrast, 70 percent of respondents in the Palestinian territories and 34 percent in Lebanon support suicide attacks.[12]

In this environment of relatively thin popular support for suicide attacks, groups may not have the luxury of selecting on quality because the supply of willing suicide attackers may be quite low. Indeed, according to data gathered during interviews of failed attackers conducted by the United Nations Assistance Mission to Afghanistan, as well as my own interviews with Afghan and international police, military, and intelligence analysts, many of the attackers are young, illiterate, and poor, persuaded to become attackers after being plucked by madaris in Pakistan's North and South Waziristan tribal agencies.

There is a tendency to assume that all suicide missions require highly competent attackers, as evidenced by the Tamil Tigers, for example. This is not likely to be true for the suicide attackers often recruited in Pakistan and employed in Pakistan and Afghanistan. For example, in Pakistan suicide attackers pursue high-value government targets, but recently suicide groups have been aiming at relatively soft targets such as police and paramilitary organizations that are more accessible to attackers, are poorly trained, and lack important technologies and transport that would make them harder to hit successfully. The same is true in Afghanistan, where international targets do comprise the largest share of successful suicide attacks (43 percent between January 1 and June 30, 2007), and attacks on Afghan security forces account for 33 percent of all attacks in the same period. (The remaining attacks are against government and other civilian targets.) However, the victim yield (defined by the number of victims per number of attackers) for attacks against Afghan forces is considerably higher than victim yields for attacks against international military targets.[13] The relatively unsophisticated attackers are most successful against police targets, which are "soft" in that they are ubiquitous, poorly armed, and in open vehicles.

In general, suicide attacks in Afghanistan are far less lethal than in any other theater, with fewer than three victims per successful suicide attack. In many cases the attacker manages to kill only himself.[14] Indeed, the reliance on young attackers from madaris may explain why suicide attacks in Afghanistan are often unsuccessful. Similarly in Pakistan, suicide attacks are most successful against the frontier constabulary and paramilitary outfits, which are also relatively accessible to attackers and poorly defended and equipped.[15]

One might expect higher-quality or higher-aptitude persons to be assigned to targets that are hardened (difficult to access, well-protected, developed sophisticated denial techniques), high-value (government officials, military forces, intelligence operatives, high-level foreigners), or for which the opportunity costs of failure are high. In the case of South Asia one would expect higher-quality militants to be deployed to Kashmir or to India proper, where the rigors of infiltration and maintaining operation security impose numerous incentives upon militant groups to select and employ the higher-quality operatives for these missions. (This expectation is confirmed in some measure by my convenience sample of Kashmir-based militants.) In contrast, Afghanistan has been a relatively easy theater in which to operate, particularly before the entry of the United States and its allies following the onset of Operation Enduring Freedom in October 2001. Infiltration into Afghanistan is easier and the requirements for operational security (language, for example) are much less demanding than in the Kashmir and Indian theaters. Thus, this theater might have required lower-aptitude persons, particularly before 2005 when the tactics of the insurgents in Afghanistan began to evolve rapidly.

During economic downturn, more-qualified, better-educated individuals may also find themselves unemployed or underemployed, and this may result in an expanded recruiting market for militant organizations. As the opportunity costs of participating in terrorism (or other illegal activity, for that matter) for higher-quality persons decline in times of economic hardship, the numbers of such higher-aptitude individuals may increase during such periods.[16] Militant groups that impose recruitment standards can choose among the available sources of willing labor power—some of whom are high-quality individuals. Thus, even if poor or uneducated persons may be disproportionately likely to want to be terrorists, groups need not hire them if higher-quality recruits (those who are more educated or accomplished in other jobs and pursuits) are available.

In Pakistan, even if madrassah students were more interested in joining these groups (a claim for which there is scant, if any, evidence), this would not mean that militant groups would have to take them when more qualified candidates were available. If this argument has any validity, substantially increasing employment opportunities may not diminish the ability of terrorist groups to operate altogether because they can lower their recruitment standards. However, such interventions may reduce the quality of terrorists available to organizations and the quality of terrorist attacks they can perpetrate.

A Critique of the Supply-side Studies

Before concluding that socioeconomic concerns as well as educational attainment and type of education acquired are irrelevant in the militancy puzzle and, therefore, that madaris have no connection to militancy, it is important to understand supply-side analyses' meaning and limitations. Several types of sample biases limit each of the above-noted studies. The individual militants in these scholars' data sets represent the outcomes of several layers of filtering or selection that result in various kinds of biases in the data. One layer is self-selection. This occurs at the onset, when the aspiring militant approaches an organization offering his or her services in exchange for group affiliation. The organization performs a second kind of selection when it decides whether or not to accept the services of the applicant. Third, once the group makes an offer to the individual, he or she may elect to join the group or drop out of the process altogether. During this vetting process both group and recruit are vulnerable to various kinds of risk and exposure.

Finally, to be included in several of the above-noted researchers' data, the individual must be successful in an operation (a suicide operation in some cases) or at least be observed to have attempted an operation. For Sageman, the operative simply must have executed or attempted to execute an attack. It is important to realize that as a result of sample biases, these studies cannot claim to generalize about the characteristics of the entire population of militants, much less the population of *willing* and *aspirant* militants. Rather, they can claim only to examine the characteristics of terrorists who have emerged from the various selection processes that result in their inclusion in a particular data set for analysis. Thus, it is far too early to dismiss links in education and socioeconomic status with the total supply of terrorist labor.[17]

Demand for Terrorism: Reasons for Concern

One serious shortcoming of the supply-side studies is that they can cast light only on those who have been observed to become militants, not the entire set of persons who want to become militants. Another lacuna is that they tend not to consider the relationship between education and socioeconomic standing and the demand for terrorism. Here demand refers to the preferences for the product of militant groups (terrorist attacks) or the support that these groups enjoy among the people on whose behalf they claim to operate.[18] The extant studies of militant labor supply do not cast light on the relationship (if any) between educational attainment, kind of education obtained, and other aspects of socioeconomic status and popular support for terrorism. Even if efforts to improve employment and quality of education and to diminish socioeconomic inequities do little in the short term to diminish the supply of militant labor resources, it is possible that such interventions may reduce demand or support for terrorism. In other words, the extant empirical literature has not attempted to examine the determinants of the support that militancy and militants garner among the population on whose behalf militant organizations claim to act and from whom their cadres and commanders are drawn.[19]

In the case of Pakistan and its religious schools, even if few militants seem to come from madaris it is still possible that madaris produce students who are more likely than students in mainstream schools to support militancy. The fact that groups select on quality filters out the underqualified madrassah students, as long as more-qualified persons are available. As I argue, there *are* madrassah students who would be high-quality, have studied in mainstream schools, and could pass through the quality filter of a terrorist organization. And for some groups, madrassah education may even confer operational benefits, especially if acquired alongside a mainstream education through which the recruit could become literate and numerate.

Indeed, some data suggest that madrassah students have a greater taste for jihad than students in the other educational streams. Tariq Rahman's survey work provides important—albeit limited—insights into the relationship between the kind of education received and attitudes toward and support for militancy in Pakistan. He administered an attitudinal survey to 488 tenth-grade students in Urdu-medium public schools, English-medium private schools, and their equivalents in madaris.[20]

He inquired about their views toward open war with India, support for various jihadist groups, and the utility of peaceful means to resolve conflicts. He also asked students whether they favored equal rights for Pakistan's religious minorities (Ahmediyas, Hindus, and Christians) and women.[21] Rahman administered a similar survey to the students' teachers as well.[22] The aggregate data for questions asked of students and teachers are in Table 9.

His results demonstrate that madrassah students are consistently more likely than students in private or public schools to support war with India and militants in Kashmir and are less likely to support equal rights for Pakistan's minorities and women. Students at private schools—where English is the primary language—are more likely to support peaceful outcomes and minority and women's rights. Public-school students' views fall between these two extremes. Thus one of the conclusions that can be drawn from this work is that although it is likely that Pakistan's madaris do not contribute significantly to the supply of terrorist labor resources, they may foster conditions conducive to support for terrorism.

However, such a conclusion is premature. As with other studies, Rahman's survey also suffers from a number of important data limitations. It is easy to attribute the observed attitudinal differences to the type of school attended, but it is also possible that the type of school attended is symptomatic and not causal. In other words, parents probably select schools that reflect their values. For example, more-liberal parents may choose private schools over other options, whereas conservative parents may prefer to use madaris for their children's education. If this reasoning is correct, the observed attitudes of children in those schools may be just as much a product of their family environment as of the school environment.[23]

However, recall from the Andrabi study that the majority of families (nearly 75 percent of madrassah households) that use a madrassah to educate at least one child fulltime also use public or private schools to educate their other children. This suggests that for most madrassah households, it is enough to have one child enrolled in a madrassah. For the majority of madrassah households, ideology may not be the primary factor explaining school choice. However, for the remaining 25 percent who put all their children in madaris for full-time education, consonance between family values and the madrassah environment may be an important consideration.

These empirical limitations do not diminish the value of this study but they must be kept in mind because they have policy implications: Simply switching children from one medium to another (such as from a madrassah to a private school) may not produce meaningfully different worldviews in students who switch educational streams. Although Rah

Table 9. Student Responses (Teacher Responses in Parentheses)

Question: What should be Pakistan's priorities?	Percent Responding	Madrassah	Urdu-Medium	English-Medium
Take Kashmir away from India by an open war	Yes	60 (70)	40 (20)	26 (26)
	No	32 (22)	53 (70)	65 (65)
	Don't Know	8 (7)	7 (10)	9 (9)
Take Kashmir away from India by supporting jihadi groups to fight the Indian army	Yes	53 (59)	33 (19)	22 (38)
	No	32 (27)	45 (68)	60 (51)
	Don't Know	15 (11)	22 (13)	17 (11)
Support Kashmir cause through peaceful means only (no war or sending of jihadi groups across the Line of Control)	Yes	34 (30)	76 (85)	72 (60)
	No	55 (67)	18 (10)	19 (34)
	Don't Know	11 (4)	6 (5)	9 (6)
Give equal rights to Ahmedis in all jobs, etc.	Yes	13 (4)	47 (27)	66 (43)
	No	82 (96)	37 (65)	9 (37)
	Don't Know	5 (NIL)	16 (8)	25 (20)
Give equal rights to Pakistani Hindus in all jobs, etc.	Yes	17 (15)	47 (37)	78 (62)
	No	76 (85)	43 (58)	14 (26)
	Don't Know	7 (NIL)	10 (5)	8 (12)
Give equal rights to Pakistani Christians in all jobs, etc.	Yes	18 (19)	66 (52)	84 (82)
	No	73 (78)	27 (42)	9 (11)
	Don't Know	8 (4)	9 (6)	8 (8)
Give equal rights to men and women as in Western countries	Yes	17 (4)	75 (61)	91 (78)
	No	77 (97)	17 (33)	6 (14)
	Don't Know	6 (NIL)	7 (6)	3 (8)

Source: Rahman, "Pluralism and Intolerance in Pakistani Society," 29.

man's work does not provide conclusive proof of causality, it does suggest that students in public schools and religious schools are more inclined than those in private schools to support jihad against India and even open war with India. This may result in students who go on to build families that also espouse these sentiments. Even if madaris do not supply the bulk of Pakistan's militants under prevailing recruitment conditions for militant groups, they may help foster communities of support for various kinds of militancy.

More Reasons for Concern: Madaris and Sectarian Violence?

As discussed throughout this volume, madrassah education is inherently sectarian, in that its principal objective is to produce students who share and agree with the sectarian worldview espoused by a particular board. One of the elemental features of madrassah education is what madrassah administrators now call "comparative religion." In practice, this involves comparing and contrasting one interpretative school vis-à-vis another, for example Sunni vs. Shia, or Deobandi vs. Barelvi. It also involves radd, or refutation, whereby students learn to counter the arguments of a sectarian system and defend their own tradition's worldview.[24]

Pakistani governmental officials and, indeed, religious scholars are concerned about the sectarianism imparted through madrassah education because of the sanguinary nature of sectarian violence in Pakistan.[25] It should be clear, however, that until now Shia-Sunni violence has meant Deobandi groups attacking Shia. Inter-Shia violence, such as that between Deobandis and Barelvis, also goes on. In the 1980s Shia militant groups received the largesse of Tehran, but they have been decimated. However, episodic counterattacks do take place on Deobandi leadership. All of the primary anti-Shia militant groups are Deobandi in orientation and take their cues from Deobandi ulama. The connections between Deoband madaris and the anti-Shia militant group, Sipah-e-Sahaba-e-Pakistan (SSP), are well known. The SSP was founded by a Deobandi cleric named Haq Nawaz Jhangvi from the city of Jhang in the Punjab. SSP cadres emerged from Deobandi madaris throughout the Punjab and Sindh.[26]

While history suggests such links between key Deobandi madaris and sectarian groups and sectarian violence, few empirical studies have examined this phenomenon. In one (problematic) study, Saleem Ali marshaled evidence to support his argument that the strongest link between madaris and violence is in the arena of sectarian activity. Employing data collected on madrassah intensity and sectarian violence from Ahmedpur (a rural area with substantial madrassah concentration and a known history of sectarian violence) and Islamabad (a highly urbanized capital with a growing madrassah concentration), Ali found that sectarian activity was positively correlated with madrassah density (madaris per unit population) in the areas he examined.[27]

Unfortunately, his sample was not adequately constructed to advance this claim. To fully measure the relationship between madrassah concentration and sectarian violence, Ali should have collected comparable data for all four kinds of regions (high madrassah concentration and high sectarian violence; high madrassah concentration and low sectarian violence; low madrassah concentration and low sectarian violence; and low madrassah concentration and high sectarian violence). These criteria for data collection are onerous and difficult in contemporary Pakistan. For this reason, even though Ali's data constitute merely a convenience sample, his findings are still provocative and demand future inquiry, if only because of the magnitude of sectarian violence in Pakistan and the hundreds of lives it claims each year.[28]

Conclusion

Extant research finds that madrassah products may not be well represented in the ranks of the observed Islamist militant groups in Pakistan; nor are they prominent among international terrorist organizations. One should not conclude, however, that madaris do not contribute to the militancy problem. Clearly, madaris in Pakistan's tribal areas provide suicide attackers in Afghanistan. Unfortunately, research that examines the characteristics of known militants cannot easily be generalized to the entire population of persons who aspire to become militants, because the latter are not easily identified for empirical inquiry. This is because militant groups, like all hirers of labor, have the luxury of selecting on quality when recruitment conditions are favorable.

As long as there are more persons wanting to join the group than actual openings, the group can continue to impose quality constraints upon its recruitment and selection process. When the group cannot meet its recruitment mission, it can relax these standards of quality. It remains very much an open question as to whether students from madaris wish to join militant groups at a higher rate than students at other kinds of schools. This is because we rarely observe the madrassah student in these groups: The Islamist militant groups in Pakistan need not take the madrassah student when the evidence suggests they have better candidates at their disposal. Thus supply-side deterrent measures may not entirely diminish the ability of groups to recruit and operate, but these measures may affect the quality of recruits who are available and the related quality of terror that these groups can produce.

If the impacts of supply-side interventions on the ability of militant groups to operate are poorly defined and difficult to measure, so are the impacts of efforts to influence the demand for terrorism. In fact, efforts to deter and deny militant groups the ability to operate (such as coun-terterrorism measures) probably *increase* the support that militant groups have among the population on whose behalf they claim to oper-ate. For example, in Pakistan enagement in Operation Silence against Islamist radicals in the Lal Masjid, work/cooperation with the United States in the global war on terrorism, and restrictions against particular Islamists once considered "jihadis" but more recently called "terrorists" may engender hostility to the Pakistani state and its leadership and fos-ter greater sympathy for Islamist militants. In other words, supply-side efforts to restrict militant groups' abilities to operate may increase the support these groups enjoy among the population.

If madrassah products are currently not uniformly or extensively represented in the ranks of some militant groups, they do seem involved in sectarian violence and in many (but not all) suicide attacks in Afghanistan and Pakistan, as described herein. Moreover, madaris likely foster demand for terrorism and may nurture communities that support the groups that perpetrate it. Important evidence also links madaris to sectarian terrorism in Pakistan.

Given that madaris have a small market share of the educational market, may have made a limited contribution of persons to militancy writ large in Pakistan, and have little actual connection to international terrorism, it is tempting to conclude that they have unnecessarily attracted the attention of international capitals. Although this is almost certainly the case, madaris *do* merit continued scrutiny, both because they probably foster communities that support terrorism in Pakistan and the region and because of their links to sectarian and suicide terrorism. Moreover, that madrassah products do not prominently figure in militant organizations operating in difficult theaters may simply be a result of selection bias: Groups that need high-quality operatives and that have the luxury of choosing need not take poorly qualified madrassah students. As conditions in Pakistan evolve, the individuals available for militant groups in Pakistan may also change. In the future more militants may come from madaris if higher-quality individuals become less available for recruitment or if militant operations in Pakistan (and Afghanistan) evolve so that they have an expressed need for madrassah students, as shown by the supply of suicide attacks.

In fact, there may be evidence that this happening. As Pakistan has dramatically shut down operations in Kashmir, suicide attacks in Pakistan have increased dramatically. As different groups engage in different operations, we may expect that militant labor demands may evolve toward ever greater reliance on madaris for recruits. For these myriad reasons, madaris require thoughtful attention, even though the larger features of Pakistan's educational landscape merit greater focus.

4

Government Reforms

As noted above, madaris have gained the attention of both international actors and Pakistan's government. Often, but not always, under significant international pressure, the government has initiated various rounds of madrassah reform. Pakistani and foreign observers alike have remarked on the seemingly limited progress of these efforts. Pakistani authorities and madrassah officials have differing opinions of their success.

The Government View

Even before the 2001 terrorist attacks, then Chief Executive Musharraf sought to reform Pakistan's system of religious education. These efforts were reinvigorated by Musharraf's alliance with the United States-led global war on terrorism, the fallout of the July 7, 2005, bombings in London, and the bombers' purported links to Pakistan. It is important to note that none of the most aggressive claims linking the bombers to madaris has been substantiated. The government's objectives, as stated by officials interviewed for this study, are simple: to make a "more socially acceptable madrassah graduate with greater employment options."

Government efforts can be divided into two broad concerns: registration of madaris and regulation of the schools and their products. Numerous furtive initiatives have sought to achieve these goals. In 2001 the Pakistani government promulgated the Pakistan Madrassah Education Ordinance (PME), which called for a body to be established explicitly to accomplish the following tasks: obtain affiliation of all madaris within a particular maslak; prescribe a syllabus for worldly subjects; and establish a model "deeni madrassah," which adheres to the government's idea of what a madrassah should be.[1] This body would be headed by a government-appointed chair; a vice-chair would be nominated by the five wafaq, and each maslak would contribute one member to this body. However, it never formed because the five boards refused to participate. They objected to this proposal because they wanted to organize on their own initiative, not at the behest of the government.

As of September 2006 some progress had been made in founding an effective body to oversee reform of the religious educational sector. The Ittehad-e-Tanzimat Madaris-e-Diniya (ITMD) formed in 2005 to serve as an umbrella organization for the five wafaq, an important first step. The government hoped that it could work with the ITMD. Previously it had had no systematic contact with the wafaq to negotiate on behalf of the madrassah constituency. The ITMD was unwilling to go further because it objected to the fact that madrassah reform was based in the education ministry; in particular it objected to dealing with the education minister, retired Lt. Gen. Javed Ashraf Qazi, a former director general of Pakistan's intelligence agency, the Interservices Intelligence Directorate (ISI), and corps commander.

The ITMD preferred to initiate and direct its own efforts toward reform. Or if it had to interact with the government, it believed the religious affairs ministry should have this portfolio. Ultimately responsibility for madrassah reform was transferred from the education ministry to religious affairs.[2] According to the religious affairs secretary, the reason for the failure to get the ITMD to work with the government on a madrassah reform board was the government's fundamental hostility to madaris and Lt. Gen. Qazi's stated goal of "undoing the madaris' existence." Thus the ITMD rejected the government's call for a madrassah reform board.[3]

Some headway was made when madrassah reform was reshuffled and placed in the religious affairs ministry. The minister is Eijaz ul Haq, Zia ul Haq's son, who has unquestionable Islamist credentials and is a known defender of the madaris. The religious affairs secretary, Vakil Ahmed Khan, believes he has been able to serve as an effective intermediary between the ITMD and the government, at least partly because he is a madrassah product.[4] After taking over as secretary and assuming responsibility for madrassah reform, Khan's first recommendation to the government was that it should stop playing a direct role. Instead it should restrict itself to allowing the ministry to work with the madaris on mutually acceptable policies. He was also concerned that the government made achieving its objectives more difficult by conflating "registration with regulation."

He explained: "The government would often talk about registration and would quickly move to curriculum. At times it seemed that they only wanted to limit registration to those with a worldly curriculum." Khan's view is that this undermined the likelihood of resolving the issue of registration, which was necessary to create a reliable data set of madaris in Pakistan.[5]

Registration remains one of the first issues to be resolved before the reform board can be formed. There has been considerable misinformation about this issue. Madaris do not reflexively oppose registration. In fact, all the madaris I visited during fieldwork in Pakistan were registered when they were built. Madrassah administrators believe that registration facilitates their fundraising efforts, as 501(c)(3) status does for charitable organizations in the United States.

Until 1994 madaris generally registered under the Societies Registration Act of 1860 (SRA 1860). In 1994 then Prime Minister Benazir Bhutto imposed a ban on such registration to retard the proliferation of madaris. What resulted was explosive growth of unregistered madaris. Registration under the SRA 1860 was not an easy process. Madaris had to verify that the land they were built on was legally held (not squatted land). They had to have various certifications from the special branch of the police to ensure that the madrassah in question was not engaging in nefarious activities. Sometimes police and intelligence officials used registration to ensure that madaris would not engage in sectarian activities.[6]

When the government began to pursue registration again in 2005, it had to evaluate the trade-offs between renewing registration with a new ordinance or revising the SRA 1860. More than 6,000 madaris were registered under the SRA 1860. Promulgating a new ordinance would mean that these 6,000 would become "unregistered." Khan reasoned that a new madrassah registration law would inflame ITMD's suspicions about the government's intentions. In the end the government amended the SRA 1860 by making it obligatory for madaris to register, whereas previously such registration had been voluntary. (The ordinance now defines madaris as distinct from makatib as well.) The new law requires that madaris file a declaration pledging that there will be no sectarian teaching, no teaching of religious hatred, and no promotion of militancy. In addition, madaris will be required to file an annual education report and a balance sheet. This balance sheet will not detail the source of the income; it will report only amounts received and payable.[7]

Madrassah administrators continued to balk, however. First, they complained that the prohibition on sectarianism constrains the teaching of what they call "comparative religion" among maslaks. Second, they refused to concede that there should be no promotion of militancy, because this would be tantamount to admitting that they had promoted militancy in the past. Third, they objected to financial reporting because madaris can be lucrative enterprises and they value confidentiality in their finances. In each case the religious affairs ministry made extensive concessions to accommodate such concerns and painstakingly negotiated the phrasing of the three main commitments in the two-page registration document. With respect to financial reporting, the government dropped its demand that madaris identify the source of their funding. They need only report what they take in and what they spend. The government continued to accommodate these reservations, and registration is again proceeding.[8]

Analysts such as Touquir Shah, a former assistant commissioner responsible for registering madaris, are astonished by these developments. In Shah's view, this "fast-track" registration is an advantage for the madaris. It is much easier than the old process and requires no verification, unlike the previous registration regime. He was also critical about the religious affairs ministry's role in this process and suggested that it demonstrates weakened will on the part of the government. He was surprised to see the watered-down financial accounting provision, given that the government and the international community alike suspected that outside funding was coming from countries and organizations that support Islamist militancy or espouse and therefore seek to advance an explicit Islamization agenda in Pakistan.[9]

There had been some optimism in 2006 that the registration impasse had been resolved in some measure, which motivated Khan to turn his attention to regulation. During our meeting he laid out the following plan to regulate madaris: First the government would extend the recognition of the five boards, which means they would have a formal, legal right to affiliate with madaris within their maslak. Currently this is the practice, but there is no legal basis for the legitimacy of this affiliation. Such affiliation would also permit them to issue a secondary certificate acceptable to all institutions in Pakistan for purposes of employment or additional education. Each board would be required to look at its own madaris and impose a standard curriculum for worldly subjects.

Even in 2006, Khan confided that his regulatory plan had met with resistance among madrassah administrators and teachers. Whereas the ITMD argued that each board should conduct its own examination, the government wants the ITMD to administer the exam for all boards. (This test would be for secular subjects. Each board conducts its own exams for religious subjects.) The government fears that if the wafaq of a maslak administers the examinations to its own students, that wafaq may be more lenient toward them. (In other words, it may have a conflict of interest and give its own students higher marks.) If the ITMD tests all students of all five maslaks, there will be fewer conflicts of interest and greater control of the test administration and adjudication of scores.[10]

Another point of contention between the government and the madrassah administrators and allies has been the issue of syllabus development, which has been in the portfolio of the education ministry. Khan believes that the religious affairs ministry has demonstrated its importance in the registration process, and its involvement is instrumental in the effort to persuade the madaris to accept a common syllabus. He claims that ITMD has concurred in principle with both registration and imparting worldly education. In fact he claims that the ITMD had agreed to use the Federal Islamabad Board syllabus, provided that the difference of opinion on testing could be worked out.[11]

If an agreement were to be made on testing, Khan envisioned that the Pakistan Education Madaris Board Ordinance (PEMBO) would be amended and at last put into operation. However, some organizational issues need to be resolved. First, should PEMBO go forward it will require the board members to disassociate themselves from the actual running of the madaris. Currently some members of the ITMD manage madaris, and Khan does not see how they can both manage and regulate, as this is a serious conflict of interest.

Khan anticipated some change in how the board will be constituted under the revised legislation. For instance, it will have a government-appointed chairman and representatives from the education and religious affairs ministries, as well as the Higher Education Commission. It will also include two or three eminent educationalists in both religious and worldly subjects. The board will be responsible for conducting inspections and imposing a uniform syllabus. It will have authority to grant secondary certificates.[12]

Khan acknowledged in 2006 that enormous problems continue to loom for the government effort. For instance, although madaris have accepted in principle the idea of curriculum reform, they do not have the resources to implement it. The education ministry has made funds available to madaris to hire teachers of the worldly curriculum and provide other resources for teaching worldly subjects. However, to date no ITMD madrassah has accepted the education ministry's money. All analysts, government officials as well as madrassah administrators, interviewed for this study confirmed the resistance to take these funds. Khan believes this resistance stemmed from the fact that they believe the funds are coming from the United States. Interestingly enough, Khan's suspicious are well founded. The amount allocated to Pakistan through USAID exactly equals the funding pledged by the government to the religious sector.

Khan also noted that the financial autonomy of madaris is important to their independence. They have benefited from relatively little oversight and would like to keep it that way. In addition, many ITMD officials are also politicians in the MMA as well as madrassah administrators. Because of their involvement in the constituent parties of the MMA and their high-profile role of opposing the government, they are in a compromised position. Once the ITMD makes a deal with the government and the details of the deal are leaked, they will come under pressure to deny it. Thus it is never really clear when these persons are reneging on negotiated positions or simply making political statements to placate their constituents, who oppose the Musharraf government and its efforts in these areas. In Khan's view, this compromised position accounts for various conflicting statements by the MMA about issues of madrassah reform and registration, even though the ITMD has agreed to these principles with the government.

While government officials were optimistic during my fieldwork about their ability to negotiate with the ITMD, intervening events have no doubt dampened this belief. Musharraf's lauded efforts in this direction have come to a standstill as a consequence of the July military action against the Red Mosque (Lal Masjid) and affiliated madrassah Jamia Hafsa. Madrassah officials have broken off negotiations about madrassah reform, accusing Musharraf of betrayal and holding him responsible for the assault on the two structures that resulted in the deaths of numerous seminary students they consider to be innocent. The actual death toll is disputed and ranges between sixty and several hundred. Many of the religious leaders were skeptical about Musharraf's motivations in pursuing madrassah reform, believing it was at the behest of Washington. Given Musharraf's expanding crisis of governance, increasing domestic terrorism, and increasingly strained relations with Washington, there may be decreasing reasons to be optimistic that Musharraf will accomplish any significant degree of madrassah reform. It remains to be seen whether his successor will take up this issue, given its contentiousness and political sensitivity.[13]

The Madaris' View

Officials like Khan in the religious affairs ministry were generally optimistic that registration and, eventually, regulation of the madaris would happen. A very different view came from madrassah officials interviewed for this study, and nearly all of them agreed. Many dismissed the idea that efforts were in fact under way to reform madaris. The comments of Maulana Khalid Binnori of Darul Uloom Sarhad are representative of madrassah administrators I interviewed. He opined: "There is no need for reform . . . . No one has the right to interfere in our institutions." Regarding the proposed changes and their impacts, he said, "These will only be cosmetic."[14] (It is worth noting that he is on the executive council of the NWFP branch of the JUI-Fazlur Rehman (JUI-F) and is the vice president of the NWFP branch of JUI-F. His daughter is also a minister in the national assembly with JUI-F.)

Many interviewees at madaris linked the purported government interest "in interfering in the business of madaris" with pressure from the United States and the United Kingdom, and most thought the government's efforts were either farcical or fictional and intended for international consumption. Few entertained the possibility that the government's efforts were sincere or well informed. The views of Maulana Taqi

Usmani of Darul Uloom Karangi Town (Karachi) typified this senti-
ment. When asked about government reforms, he quipped, "Are there
any?" He dismissed the efforts of the government as cosmetic.

He commented: "They raise slogans in different circles that they are
reforming madaris and that reform of madaris is needed. They are not
clear about what these reforms are that they want. We are institutions
that are criticized from all directions [by persons who have not studied
our system]. [These proposed changes] are imaginary concepts that
have developed in different circles, and this is the foundation of the criticism [of our system]."[15]

Many madrassah administrators see no need to introduce worldly
subjects into their curriculum for two reasons. First, some have already
expanded their curriculum. As one administrator at Darul Uloom
Islamiya (Lahore) remarked: "We have already reformed by ourselves.
We are ten years ahead of the government. What they are now saying,
we did ten years ago. We don't agree with their notion of liberalism.
Islam has no notion of liberalism. Religion is as it was—it doesn't
change." This madrassah has a high-school program (sixth to tenth
grade) that mixes worldly and religious subjects.

Administrators at Kher ul Madaris, which has an extensive, seventeen-
year curriculum combining both worldly and religious education,
explained: "Regarding Nisab [syllabus], the government says that madaris
do not have secular education. But this isn't true here. Large madaris
only take students that are matriculates [tenth-grade graduates]. We
have already imposed this, and this means that our students have a secular education. We also have introduced secular subjects." But he conceded that small madaris, which make up the majority of madaris in
Pakistan, do not have the resources for such standards.[16]

Second, as suggested above, schools that do not have worldly subjects
in their curriculum (the majority visited) discount the need for an
expanded curriculum because they claim to admit only students with an
eighth- or tenth-grade qualification. Such opponents of reform argue
that in Pakistan students begin to specialize only after the tenth grade.
Thus, in their view, madrassah education is a kind of specialization. To
require madaris to introduce math and engineering, in their opinion, is
akin to asking medical schools to introduce Islamic studies.

An administrator at Jamia Mantazir stated clearly that they "do not agree with whatever program the government has started." But "to some extent we do agree that madrassah students should have some secular education. However, to the extent that this means that we include those subjects in the madrassah curriculum, we disagree. We are a postmatriculation specialization that goes on top of a basic educational foundation. Our first priority is the provision of religious studies. If they want to study other subjects, they can."

Maulana Hafez Khalil Ahmad of Jamia Matla-ul-Uloom (Quetta) runs a madrassah that neither imposes strict requirements for matriculation nor uses an expanded curriculum. Nonetheless, he opposes government reforms. He noted, "The government is unable to effect change in the curriculum and it probably will not. If Musharraf forces us, we will push back; there will be a clash."[17]

Madrassah administrators are also irritated by the registration issue. They view this as a problem the government has created. They noted that they themselves are already registered, and that madaris actually want to register at least partly because, as noted above, registration assists with their fundraising efforts. An administrator at Kher ul Madaris explained: "The big madaris have already been registered. No one has any objection to registration. It is the words that have been added to the registration declaration that is the problem. There is no deadline for the registration."[18]

An administrator at Binnori Town agreed that most are already registered but noted that now "the government wants to make the process more difficult."[19] (A former official who did the registration, Touquir Shah, derides this view.)[20] This administrator says that at the core, they do not trust the government and see its registration effort as insincere and ultimately a means to interfere in madaris with the aim of de-Islamizing Pakistan's educational system.[21] He is correct in his general assessment.[22]

Madrassah administrators have no interest in taking government money for program expansion. They like the current situation, in which "they take nothing from the government, and the government therefore has no grounds to interfere."[23] They fear that should they accept government funding for anything, then they will be vulnerable to its interference. Madrassah administrators are similarly irritated over Musharraf's claim that foreign students were expelled from the madaris and from Pakistan to placate Washington and other capitals that believed Pakistan's madaris cultivate foreign terrorists. Madrassah administrators and teachers explained that in fact it was not an expulsion of foreign students. Rather, the interior ministry only gave a suggested date of voluntary departure for these students. Madrassah administrators claim there is no evidence that the students were or are involved in illegal activities; they said they believe students who break the law should be expelled.

These views do not hold up under strict scrutiny. The younger brother of Hambali, al Qaeda's organizer in Southeast Asia and mastermind of the Bali blasts, was arrested along with seventeen people from Malaysia, Indonesia, and Burma in raids on three madaris in Karachi.[24] I did confirm during fieldwork that substantial numbers of foreign students from Africa, Europe and the United Kingdom, the Middle East, and Central, South, and Southeast Asia were at many of the madaris I visited. In fact Jamia Binoria SITE (Karachi) still has a large foreign-students' section, and one can still visit its Web site to obtain information about applying for the foreign students' program.[25]

The Islamic Scholars' View

I also met with scholars at the Council of Islamic Ideology, the director general of the Islamic Research Institute at the International Islamic University (IIU) Islamabad, and the president of the Islamic University Islamabad. They all understood the hesitation of the madaris and the numerous—seemingly insurmountable—challenges in madrassah reform, but most conceded that the quality of Islamic education has been in a state of decline for "centuries." They noted that the public educational system in Pakistan is also in decline with out-of-date methods (rote), a problematic curriculum, poorly trained teachers, bad textbooks, and inadequate facilities. They believe that madrassah teachers, administrators, andproponents understand the need for reform. Dr. S.M. Zaman and Dr. Mahmood Ghazi of IIU noted that the current system produces ulama who are not relevant to the modern Muslim state of Pakistan. Ghazi even conceded that although madaris may not be producing transnational terrorists, they have contributed to the menace of sectarian violence and an obscurantist worldview in Pakistan.[26] Several religious scholars interviewed for this work also expressed concern that the ulama that emerge from these madaris are simply ill-equipped to guide the modern Islamic state that Pakistan aspires to be.

Conclusion

The Pakistani government's efforts to reform the madrassah sector and the resistance of the madrassah community to these efforts are poorly understood outside Pakistan. Contrary to popular belief, the government *had been* making headway, and many of the madaris' concerns have less to do with their recalcitrant clinging to institutions that support militancy and more to do with protecting entrenched institutional and familial interests. However, there is little doubt that Musharraf's declining legitimacy and concomitant crisis of governance, increased state confrontation with Islamist militants, deepening hostility to the United States across all segments of Pakistani society, and Musharraf's alliance with Washington have culminated in a serious derailment of these efforts. Ironically, it is precisely these issues that have impressed upon Musharraf the increasing need to contend with Pakistan's madrassah-related problems. Unfortunely, he is less and less inclined to make or even incapable of making significant headway in reforming the madaris.

Nonetheless, in my interviews in 2006, there was a striking difference between the views of the government and those of the madaris about the clarity of mission in madrassah reform, the progress made, and the motivation for the reform agenda. The government sees its goals as clearly defined and believes it has made definitive—albeit slow—progress. Madrassah administrators, in contrast, dismiss the government's goals as at best poorly defined and at worst a sideshow to placate Western countries obsessed with madaris. The few madrassah officials who did believe the government is serious in its efforts to reform religious education dismissed these initiatives as futile and derided them as ill-informed and unnecessary. In extreme cases, some madrassah administrators and teachers even intimated that they were prepared to resist reform violently should the government seriously undertake its stated agenda. The violence at the Lal Masjid and Jamia Hafsa reminds us that these threats should be taken seriously.

Arguably the government's motivations to reform these schools are informed by legitimate concerns about the effect of madaris on Pakistan's domestic security situation, including their connections to sectarian violence and their inability to produce ulama relevant to a modernizing Islamic state. These government views are also held by key religious scholars, suggesting a broader base of support than is often presumed to exist for these initiatives. However, while religious scholars acknowledged the importance that madaris have for the country, most interviewees believed that this issue concerns Pakistan and Pakistanis—not the international community. Furthermore, most interviews with government authorities, Islamic scholars, and madrassah officials suggested that U.S. involvement in this area has hurt more than it has helped, because it has served to delegitimize the government's efforts and reduce them to mere action items dictated by Washington and London.

5

Conclusions and Implications

Formal religious education in Pakistan generally takes place in religious educational institutions such as makatib and madaris. However, the government curriculum used in the Urdu-medium public schools also includes Islamic studies and relies heavily on a highly selective interpretation of Islam to convey other subjects such as biology, mathematics, and social sciences. Despite public perceptions to the contrary, madrassah enrollments are very low nationally and comprise less than 1 percent of all full-time school enrollments. Most school-going children (nearly 70 percent overall) attend Pakistan's government schools, and the remainder attend private schools. There is important geographical variation in the enrollments of madaris, with the greatest concentration in the Pashto-speaking areas along the Pakistan-Afghanistan border.

Although the majority of students attending madaris are from less-affluent families, overall 12 percent of madrassah students come from Pakistan's wealthiest families. For the most part, madaris are funded through private philanthropy, although their students may obtain zakat, a portion of which goes to the school to cover educational costs. The government has offered financial incentives to madaris to expand their curriculum to include worldly subjects, but so far very few credible madaris—if any—have taken advantage of these subsidies.

Limited poll data suggest that Pakistanis support some type of madrassah reform. However, other poll data over multiple years suggest that Islam plays a prominent and welcome role in public life in Pakistan. (A sizable portion of Pakistanis do believe that Islam's role in Pakistan's public life is too prominent.) Interview data, albeit anecdotal, suggest a resurgence of support for and interest in Islamic education in Pakistan generally. Buttressing interlocutors' views is the fact that the educational market has produced numerous innovative educational options that combine mainstream curriculum with Islamic education. Many of these schools are very expensive and have cost structures similar to those of Pakistan's elite private schools. The available evidence suggests that

Islamic education in Pakistan is in an experimental phase that may parallel in some way the development of parochial education in the United States.

Despite popular assertions that madaris are the cradles of militancy, my current and previous research has found little support for this contention. However, studies by others have found that madaris produce students who are significantly less tolerant and more inclined than counterparts in public and private schools to support violent means of resolving disputes. (Nevertheless, public school students show a high degree of intolerance compared to those in private schools.) Madaris also have been linked in some studies to sectarian violence. Pakistani officials interviewed for this study share this viewpoint; they agree that ways must be found to encourage madaris to cease imparting sectarian worldviews to their students.

While the government is pressing ahead with reforms, madrassah administrators remain staunchly opposed to these efforts. This opposition is featured in the popular press, but the reasons for it often are not. My fieldwork in Pakistan suggests that madrassah officials (many of whom have inherited their jobs, as if madrassah administration were a family business) resist change not because they are sponsors of terrorism but rather because many madaris are lucrative enterprises that have thrived without government oversight. Madrassah families want to preserve this privilege. There are also serious debates in Pakistan about the role of madaris: Should they be used as a general educational tool, or should they keep their focus on training personnel for clerical jobs and the various Islamist parties?

Data collected and synthesized herein suggest that the United States would do well at least to consider ceasing public calls for madrassah reform in Pakistan. Such statements have produced a substantial backlash in various sectors of Pakistani society and have complicated government efforts to implement a reform agenda. This does not mean that the international community should cease making quiet statements to Pakistani leadership to this effect. Pakistanis are deeply suspicious of U.S-supported efforts to reform Pakistan's public schools, as they believe the United States seeks to de-Islamize the country's educational system. (High-level officials in the U.S. State Department confirmed to me that this is, in fact, one of their goals.)[1] The United States should consider diminishing its public role and encouraging its partners and multilateral agencies to take a discreet role in these initiatives.

Implications and Policy Considerations

The extant evidence is overwhelming that madaris comprise a very small share of the full-time education market (perhaps as low as 1 percent of all full-time students). Moreover, since 1991 (the earliest date for which there are comparative data), the madrassah market share has remained stable or even declined somewhat. However, although 1 percent is a small percentage of the overall student market, small numbers can have large consequences, including sectarianism and connections to sectarian violence, the production of suicide attacks in Pakistan and elsewhere, the fostering of worldviews that are not conducive to domestic or external peaceful coexistence, and, in some isolated cases, other forms of militancy in Pakistan and beyond. Each of these aspects of the madrassah conundrum needs particular methods of redress.

Sectarianism is an unfortunate product of the madrassah system because madaris are founded on sectarian lines and their primary objective is to produce students and religious scholars capable of defending the virtues of a particular wafaq's worldview. Sectarianism does not simply mean pitting Shia against Sunni Muslims in Pakistan; it also involves differentiating along Sunni sectarian lines. This means pitting Barelvis against Deobandis as much as Sunni versus Shia. An appropriate response to this problem requires fundamental reordering of the madrassah system and its curriculum, which will involve generating consensus on the need for religious curriculum reform and religious teacher training across the five wafaq. This is a task for Pakistanis alone.

This is not tantamount to compelling madaris to secularize their curriculum. In fact, it may be best to recognize that the madaris' aim is to produce students who work in religious occupational fields and for the religious political parties. Such curriculum reform and concomitant teacher training cannot be done from the top down, the Musharraf government's preferred mode of action. Rather, such reform will involve tedious consensus building across broad swaths of Pakistan's religious elite and madrassah administrators of all levels while sustaining support for madrassah reform from above. With the current problems in Musharraf's government and expanding internal security challenges, this balancing act will become even more difficult.

Pakistan has suffered decades of sanguinary sectarian violence and should be willing to begin the process of forging consensus. Critically, even Pakistan's religious scholars acknowledge the need for madrassah curriculum reform. These scholars comprise an important bastion of support for the government's efforts to diminish the connections between religious education and sectarian violence. Pakistanis contend that this is an issue for Pakistan and insist that there is little role for the international community to play, other than finding creative ways of supporting this process without tainting it.

While the government is by most accounts committed to finding some way of diminishing sectarian violence, it is seriously compromised in one key respect. Because several of the Deobandi sectarian militant groups (such as Lashkar-e-Jhangvi) have overlapping membership with key groups (including Jaish-e-Mohammad and Harkat-ul-Jihad-Islami) claiming to operate in Kashmir and India, the Pakistani authorities have shown considerable ambivalence about completely eliminating these groups. This situation will persist as long as Pakistan feels the need to support militant groups for operations in the region.

A second concern of this research is whether students at madaris display violent worldviews. The available data render it impossible to discern whether the opinions of madrassah students are a product of the religious school, a reflection of the views of their parents and other household members, or some combination of both. Although madrassah worldviews probably are a joint product of the system and the family background of the student, the madrassah may be the best site for intervention. Again, this is a problem of domestic importance to Pakistan. To the extent that the educational environment can shape student perceptions, working with madrassah administrators and educators to reform the curriculum and spread teacher training would be helpful. Alternatively, creative financial and nonfinancial incentives to motivate parents to shift their children out of madaris into public or private schools might also be considered.

The third problem is the connection between some madaris and militant groups. In principle, this is the easiest one to dispense with because it is essentially a law-and-order problem, except in FATA, where there is no true law enforcement agency. Moreover, the madaris that have direct links to militancy are probably few in number and already known to the intelligence agencies. Some of them may be located in places such as the tribal area where Islamist fighters have waged war against Pakistani security forces since 2004. Clearly, taking action against some madaris with ties to militancy may be easier than moving against others. The real barrier to going after these madaris is the will and capabilities of the government. As long as Islamabad remains committed to using asymmetric warfare (jihad in Kashmir, India, and Afghanistan) to prosecute its foreign policy initiatives, the government will hesitate to shut down facilities associated with producing so-called jihadis. Thus far the international community has been unwilling to take the steps necessary to compel Pakistan to abandon its reliance upon jihadis.

With respect to madaris linked to militancy, a complex problem may be summarized in a few simple observations. Except in the Federally Administered Tribal Areas, at this point Pakistan can shut down many (though perhaps not all) madaris with known ties to militancy if it chooses to. The challenge to the United States and the international community is coming up with the right mix of incentives to persuade Islamabad of the virtues of closing down these madaris and reversing its decades-old policy of using jihadist proxies as instruments of foreign policy.

Worldly Education

Because madaris are "low-number, high-risk" institutions, they merit continuous monitoring and evaluation. However, the international community must not make madrassah reform the focus of its policy at the expense of other pressing educational issues. Pakistan's public schools should receive the bulk of Pakistan's and the international community's attention. This sector educates the vast majority of Pakistan's students (at least 70 percent), and available data suggest that public school students have views only marginally more accommodating of domestic and external peace than those of madrassah counterparts. The same can be said of their teachers. Most major studies of militant groups in other theaters contend that militants are educated in the public sector. Since it educates most of Pakistan's students, this sector—not madaris—is where reform efforts should take place.

These efforts should reflect an adequate understanding of parental choice. The current approaches favored by Islamabad and Washington involve greater secularization of Pakistan's various educational institutions. This seems out of synch with what Pakistani consumers appear to want. The changes in the educational market since the late 1980s reflect the ever-growing taste for religiously grounded education. Continued efforts to de-Islamize Pakistan's educational system run the risk of pushing parents further out of the public-school sector and into new schools that seek to combine worldly education with religious education, or at least provide worldly education in religious environments. It remains to be seen how students will emerge from these new schools, in terms of the quality of the education they obtain and the kind of citizens they become. However, policies that encourage parents to exit the public school system raise several kinds of as-yet-unknown concerns. These religiously oriented private schools may not be the government's allies in the production of Pakistani citizens. Public schooling everywhere provides the state with the opportunity to instill in its future constituents notions of civics, national identity, and national unity.

A better model may be found in the development of parochial education in the United States and elsewhere. The period of experimentation in education in Pakistan seems reminiscent of the phase of experimentation in the West, as Catholic, Lutheran, and other religiously motivated parents and educators struggled to provide children with an education appropriate for their societies in a morally and religiously acceptable atmosphere consistent with their faith-based worldview. This history may be illuminating for Pakistani educationalists and administrators. The experience of parochial education in the United States, Canada, and Europe may provide important models and lessons for Pakistan. This history could form the basis of important programs initiated by the international community to support ongoing educational reform efforts in Pakistan—not only in the religious sector but also in the mainstream sector.

Research presented here shows that private schools, contrary to popular opinion, educate nearly a third of Pakistan's students and cater to a wider array of social (class and rural or urban) backgrounds than usually thought. Private schools have not been associated with militancy, and compared to madaris and public schools, their students and teachers appear more tolerant and less supportive of violence. One cannot rule out the possibility that private schools attract, rather than produce, more liberal students and teachers. But private schools—especially those that teach Pakistan studies and civics classes—may be an important element in a strategy to change student worldviews. Small-scale experiments, using vouchers and other incentives to encourage parents to consider switching their school choice, may be considered when higher-quality private or public school options are available. Appropriate attitudinal testing, controlling for family environment, teacher inputs, and school effects, should be used to evaluate the impacts of moving students into a different educational stream.

Educational reform in Pakistan cannot be meaningful without addressing the fact that many parents opt out of the educational market altogether rather than send their children to madaris for full-time instruction. Various studies make a number of helpful observations. The first decision that a family makes is whether or not to enroll a child at the primary level. For girls, the most important determinant in this choice is the physical distance between the home and the school. This effect is not as strong for boys' enrollment. However, girls still will not go to school unless there are female teachers at the school. This suggests that a differentiated approach is necessary for female and male education. Simply building more schools may not be an adequate supply-side intervention.

For instance, building more numerous and smaller girls' schools with high-quality female teachers may be the best strategy to increase girls' enrollments, while larger, more centrally located boys' schools may be adequate to increase their access to education. Families will also opt out of the educational system if they perceive the quality of the education to be low, even if a school has teachers of appropriate gender. Unfortunately, the determinants of quality perception remain poorly characterized in the literature, despite the fact that this is an important part of the analytical puzzle.

The evidence suggests that although the overall attainment of Pakistani students is low, the conditional attainment is considerably higher. That is, once a family decides to enroll a child in primary school, the likelihood is strong that the child will continue into secondary education. Depending on secondary-school enrollment, a student has a high chance of continuing to higher secondary, and so forth. Notably, despite differences in girls' and boys' enrollment at lower levels, at the tertiary levels the retention rates normalize and the gender difference diminishes. This suggests that ensuring schools are available to families—at an affordable rate with quality teachers of appropriate gender—may be among the most important factors for expanding educational enrollment and attainment in Pakistan for both boys and girls. The international community can provide assistance in this area by helping expand the inventory of schools, provided that they rely upon the extant scholarship on parental choice in Pakistan to help guide the location of schools and the production of high-quality teachers of appropriate gender for these schools. It is also important for the international community to remain sensitive to what Pakistani parents want for their children's education—not what the international community wants for their children.

For families that continue to opt out of the market despite ready availability of schools with appropriate teachers, other incentives may be needed. It is possible that the family considers the opportunity costs of education (labor, domestic production, social concern) to outweigh any short- or long-term benefit. To meet economic concerns, educational planners should consider targeted incentives such as food distribution and stipends. For parents who choose not to educate girls for sociocultural reasons, social marketing and other policies aimed at altering views over time should be employed. Additional monetary and nonmonetary incentives (scholarships, food for enrollment, stipends, and so forth) may need to be considered.

There are many initiatives the United States and the international community *could* take but a smaller subset of initiatives they *should* take. In all cases, however, these interventions should follow an empirically sound assessment of the connections between education and militancy. Equally important, the various initiatives should reflect a nuanced understanding of parental choice in Pakistan, a consideration that has been lacking thus far. For example, moving to secularize schools in Pakistan will require substantial expenditures but will have little impact if parents value religious education. The market will accommodate these preferences in one way or another, especially since religious education is highly and widely valued in Pakistan, at least partly because it is seen to contribute to helping children become good Muslims.

More than five years after 9/11, the international community is still focusing on the madrassah scapegoat and remains busy formulating educational policies that demonstrate a lack of understanding of the Pakistani educational market and the aspects of education that Pakistani decision makers value. Much time and many resources have been squandered while the problems confronting Pakistan continue to proliferate.

Many U.S. government analysts I interviewed in recent years noted that collecting and analyzing such data take time. They said they often need to devise programs and allocate funding within time frames that do not afford the luxury of such data acquisition. This may be understandable bureaucratically, but the fact remains that had plans been made to collect much-needed data in late 2001 or early 2002, substantial findings would have been developed by now, and these data would have done much to guide the formulation of efficacious education policy. Although data collection indeed takes time, considerable data on these pressing issues have been collected, analyzed, and published already. But these studies seem to be largely inaccessible to most policymakers in the United States. I hope this effort will begin to fill the empirical gaps while encouraging governmental and nongovernmental analysts and scholars alike to continue such research.

Appendix A

Syllabus of Wafaq-ul-Madaris, Including Selected Radd Texts

1. Ibtidaiyah (Primary religious education)

Noorani Qaidah (Beginners' textbooks for Arabic language)
Nazirah Quran Kareem (Recitation of Quran)
Tajweed and Hafiz Part 30 Amma (Correct recitation and memorization of Quran.)
Urdu Language
Mathematics
Social Sciences
General Science
Practical Crafts
Islamiyat
Physical Training
Provincial Language
Government Primary School Curriculum

2. Mutawassitah (Middle)

Tajweed al-Quran (Correct recitation of the Quran)
Hadr (Rapid recitation of the Quran)
Ilm-ul-Tajweed (The science of Quranic phonetics)
Persian Language
Calligraphy
Aqaid (Beliefs)
Ibadaats (Acts of worship)
Muamalat (Business Practice, Transactions)
Morality and Character
Social Sciences
Urdu Language
Mathematics

Science
English

3. Thanviyah-e-Aammah (Secondary)

Dars-i-Nizami
Qirrah (Phonetically modulated recitation of the Quran)
Tafseer-ul-Quran (Exegesis)
Hadith Nabawi (Sayings of the Holy Prophet)
Nahw (Syntax)
Sarf (Morphology)
Arabic Literature
Fiqh (Islamic Jurisprudence)
Mantiq (Logic)

4. Thanaviyah-e-Kassah (Higher Secondary)

Tafseer ul-Quran (Exegesis)
Hadith Nabawi
Fiqh (Jurisprudence)
Usul-ul-Fiqh (Principles of Jurisprudence)
Nahw (Syntax)
Sarf (Morphology)
Mantiq (Logic)
Arabic Literature

5. Aaliyah (Bachelors)

Tafseer-ul-Quran (Exegesis)
Hadith Nabawi
Ilm-ul-Faraid (Science of Inheritance)
Usul-ul-Fiqh
Ilm-ul-Balaghah (Rhetoric)
Arabic Literature
Logic
Philosophy
Arabic Composition
Ilm-ul-Jadi (Munaziarah, or Debate)
Ilm-ul-Kalam (Scholastics)
Ilm-ul-Arud (Prosody)

6. Alimiyah (Master's)

Taseer-ul-Quran (Exegesis)
Usul-ul-Tafseer (Principles of Exegesis)
Ilm-ul-Hadith (Knowledge of the sayings of Holy Prophet.)
Usul al-Hadith (Principles of Hadith)
Fiqh
Usul al-Fiqh
Ilm-ul-Kalam (Scholastics)
Ilm-ul-Hai'at (Astronomy)
Islam
Modern economy and business, etc.

Selected Radd (Refutation) Texts

* Mohammad Yusuf Ludhianwi, *Ikhtilafe-Ummat aur Sirat-e-Mustaqim*. Karachi: Maktaba Ludhianwi, 1995.

* Syed Abul Hasan Ali Nadvi. N.D., *Muslim Mamalik Mein Islamiat our Maghribiat Ki Kash Makash*. Karachi: Majlis-e-Nashriat-e-Islam, no date.

* Mohamad Manzur Nomani, *Futuhat-e-Nomania: Manzir-e-Ahl-e-Sunnat*. Lahore: Anjuman-e-Irshad ul Muslameen, 2002.

* Arshad ul Qadri, *Zalzala*. Lahore: Shabbir Brothers, 1998.

* Muhammad Hidayat ul Qasim, *Shi'a*. Multan: Taleefat-e-Ashrafiya, no date.

* Muhammad Rafi Usmani, *Europe Ke Teen Muashi Nizam*. Karachi: Idara-ul-Muarif, 1997.

* Mohammad Zikria, *Fitna-e-Maudoodiat*, Lahore: Maktaba ul Qasim, 1975.

Source: Derived from *Social Development in Pakistan Annual Review 2002–03, The State of Education* (Islamabad: SPDC, 2003), 173–74. http://www.spdc-pak.com/publications/sdip2003.asp.

Appendix B

Arabic Texts Used in Dars-i-Nizami, Organized by Subject

All books below are in Arabic.

Tafseer (Quran Studies—Exegesis)		
Book Name	**Author**	**Year of Author's Death (CE)**
Quran		
Tafseer Bezawi/Anwar ul tanzeel	Abdullah Bin Umar Bezavi	1286
Tafseer Ibn Kaseer	Ammad uddin Ibn Kaseer	1373
Tafseer Mudaarik Al tanzeel	Abu Albarkat Abdulla Nasfi	1310
Tafseer Jalaaleen	Jalaal Uldeen Mahali	1459
Tafseer	Jalaal Uldeen Seyuti	1505
Tafsser Mazhri	Sanaullah Paanipati	1810
Alfawz ak-kabeer	Shah Wali Alladahlvi	1762
Shaatbiya (Qaseed alaamiya)	Muhammad Bin Khalaf Shaatbi	1194
Muqadima Jazariya	Shamas Muhammad Jazari	1429
Fawaaid Makkiya	Abdul Rehman	1911
Khilaasa Ab-bayaan	Ziauddeen Nara	1854
Altaisir Fit-tafseer	Najam Uddin Umar Nafsi	1142
Tafseer Kishaaf	Jaarulla Zamakhshari	1377

Hadith va Uloom-e-Hadith (Hadith and the Study of Hadiths)		
Mowtaa	Imaam Malik	795
Mowtaa Imam Muhammad	Muhammad Bin Hassan Sheebani	805
Sahih Bukhari	Muhammad Bin Ismaeel Bukhari	870
Sahih Muslim	Abu Ulhusain Muslim Neeshapuri	875
Sunin Abu Dawood	Abu Daood Sulaiman Sajastani	889
Sunan Ibn Maajah	Muhammad Bin Yazeed Qazveeni	887
Jaama Tirmizi	Muhammad Bin Isa Tirmizi	892
Sunan Nasaye	Abu Abdul Rehman Ahmad Nasayee	915
Maane Ul-Aasaar (Tahaawi)	Abu Jafar Ahmed Tehaavi	933
Mushkil Allasaar	Abu Jafar Ahmad Tahaavi	933
Musaabih	Hussain Fara Baghawi	1122
Mishkaat ul Musaabih	Wali uddin Khateeb Iraqi	1339
Fatah Ab-bari	Ahmed Ibn Hajar Asqalani	1449
Muqaddima Ibn ussalaah	Taqi uddin Ibn Salaah	1245
Nakhbat ul-fikr	Ahmed Ibn Hajar Asqalani	1449
Shamail Tirmizi	Muhammad bin Isa Tirmizi	892

Uloom Fiqh (Jurisprudence)

Mukhtasar al-Qadoori	Abul Hasan Ahmed Quduri	1037
Bidaya Awlein	Barhaanuddeen Ali Marghinani	1197
Kanz ad-duqaayiq	Abu Al Barkaat Abdulla Nasafi	1310
Sharih waqaayat Arrwwaiyah	Abaidulla Bin Masud Bukhari	1346
Nur Ul ayzaah	Hassan Ammaar Vafai	1658
Al Muntakhib Alhisaami	Hasaamuddeen Muhammad Farghani	1237
Minar ul-Anwaar	Abul Barkaat Abdulla Nasafi	1310
Assowl Ash-shaashi	Nizamuldeen Shaashi Qandi	1353
At-tanqeeh wa Towzeeh	Abdullah Bin Masud Bukhari	1346
Talweeh Sharah Towzeeh	Saad uddeen Masud Taftaazani	1390
Muslim as-Saboot	Qazi Muhibulla Bihaari	1707
Sharah Muslim as-Saboot	Abdulhaq Khairaabaadi	1899
Nura Anwaar	Sheikh Ahmed Mulla Jeevan Imeethi	1718
Siraajiyeh/Siraaji	Siraajuddeen Sajaadandi	11th Century C.E.
Hajjat ab-Baligheh	Shah Wali ullah Dehlvi	1762
Ash-shabaa wa anazaair	Zainuddeen Ibn Najeem	1561
Aqood rasama Al Mufti	Muhammad Amin bin Aabdin	1836
Dirra-Mukhtar	Allauddeen	1677

Aqaaid (Principles of Faith - Theology)

Aqeedat attahaawiyeh	Abu Jafar Ahmed Tahaavi	933
Aqaaid an-Nasfe	Najamuddeen Umar Nasafi	1142
Sharah Aqaaid Nasfi	Saaduddeen Taftazaani	1390
Masaaira fil Aqaa'id	Kamaaluddin Ibn Alhaam	1411
Hawaash Sharah Aqaaid, Khayaali	Shamsuddeen Ahmad Khyali	1465
Musaamarah	Kamaaluddin Abu Almaali	1499
Amuuri–Aame	Muhammad Zahid Harvi	1699
Sharah Muwaaqif	Mir Sharif Ali Jarjani	1413
Sharah Aqaaid Jalaali	Jalaaluddin Dawani	1502

Adab (Literature)

Siba Mualliqaat	Hammaad ul Raawia	772
Diwan Himmaasah	Habeeb Bin Ustayi	846
Diwan Mutanabbi	Ahmed Bin Hussain Mutannabi	1009
Muqaamaat Hariri	Qaasim Hariri	1122
Nafhat al Yaman	Ahmed Yamani Sharwaani	1840
Mufeed at-taalibein	Muhammad Ahsan Naanautwi	1894
Nafhat al-Arab	Muhammad Azaaz Ali	1955

Ilm ul Sarf (Grammar)

Meezaan as-Sarf	Siraajuddin Usman Awadhi	1357
Munshab	Hameeduddin Kakorvi	1801
Shaafiyeh	Jamaaluddin ibn Hajib	1248
Sarfi-Mir	Mir Shareef Ali Jarjani	1413
Panj Ganj	Siraajuddin Usman Awadhi	1357
Ilm as-Seegheh	Inaayat Ahmad Kakorvi	1862
Marah al-Arwah	Ahmad bin Ali bin Masud	?
Fasooli Akbari	Qazi Ali Akbar Alahbaadi	1679
Mayatul Aamil	Abdul Qahir Jarjani	1079

Ilm un Nahv (Grammar)

Kaafiyeh	Jamaluddeen Usman Hajib	1248
Bidayet an-nahou	Siraajuddeen Usman Chishti	?
Nahou Mir	Mir Shareef Ali Jarjaani	1413
Sharah Maaya Aamil	Hassamuddin Hussain Nauqaani	1519
Sharah Maat Aamil	Sheikh Abdur Rehman Jaami	1446
Sharah Kaafiyeh	Sheikh Abdur Rehman Jaami	1446
Tas-heel ak-kafiyeh	Abulhaq Khairaabadi	1899

Ilm-e-Maani wa Beyaan (The Study of Meaning and Exegesis)

Talkhees al-Muftaah	Jalaaluddeen Muhammad Qazvini	1338
Mukhtasar Ul Maani	Saaduddeen Masud Taftazaani	1390
Matoul	Saaduddeen Masud Taftazaani	1390
Bahas Faal ibn Aqeel	Abdullah Ahmad Ibn Aqeel	1396
Sharah Jaamee	Sheikh Abdul Rehman Jaami	1446
Hishayet Sharah Jaamee	Abdul Ghafoorlaari	1506

Ilm-e-Uruuz (Knowledge of Poetic Forms)

Uruuz ilmiftaah	Yousaf Bin Abibakar Sakaaki	1339

Ilm-e-Mantaq (Logic)

As-seeyaaghaji-Qula aqoul	Aseeruddeen Umar Abhari	1261
Shamsiyyeh	Najamuddeen Ali Dabeer	1276
Qutbi-Sharah Shamsiyyeh	Muhammad Qutabuddeen Tehtaani	1364
Mir Qutbi (Sharah Qutubi)	Mir Shreef Ali Jarjaani	1413
Tah-zeeb al-Mantaq	Saaduddeen Masud Taftazani	1390
Sughra Kabra	Mir Shareef Ali Jarjani	1413
Sharah Tah-zeeb	Abdulla Yazdi	1606
Salim al-uloom	Qaazi Muhibullah Bihari	1707
Sharah Tasdeeqaat salim	Hamadullah Sandelvi	1785
Qazi Mubaarik	Mohammad Mubaarak Gopaamvi	1794
Sharih Mulla Hassan	Mula Hassan Lakhnowi	1794
Marqaat	Fazal Imam Khair Aabaadi	1828
Tassawaraat Sharah Muslim	Qazi Mubaarak Gopaamui	1730
Risaalat Mir Zaid	Mir Muhammad Zahid Harvi	1690

Fun Manaazara (The Art of Argumentation—Polemics)

Shareefeeyah	Mir Shareef Ali Jarjaani	1413
Rasheedeeyah	Abdulrasheed Deevaan Jaunpuri	1672

Falsafa (Philosophy)

Bidayet ul-hakmiyah	Aseeruddeen Abhari	1261
Meeb-zi	Mir Hassan Meebzi	1685
Sadra haasheeya	Sadaruddeen Sheeraazi	1641
Shams Baazghah	Mahmood bin Muhammad Junpuri	1652
Bidaayeh Saeediyeh	Fazal-e-Haq Khairaabaadi	1861

Hait-wa-hindsa (Astronomy and Arithmetic)

Malkhas Chagmeeni	Sharfuddeen Chaqmeeni Khwarzmi	1221
Sharih Chagmeeni	Musa Qaazizaada Rumi	1411
Tashreeh al-Aflaak	Bahauddeen Muhammad Aamli	1622
Tashreeh Sharih Tashreeh al-Aflaak	Imaamuddeen Lahori	1732
Khilaasah fi al-hisaab	Bahauddeen Muhammad Aamli	1622
Bistibaab Aqleedis	Naseeruddeen Muhqiq Tusi	1274

Tibb (Medicine/medical)

Al Qanoon	Hakeem Abu Ali Seena	1037
Qaanoonchah	Sharafuddeen Khwaarzmi	1221
Sharah Asbaab	Burhaanuddeen Nafees Karmaani	1438
Mawjiz	Alauddeen Qarshi	1288

Tareekh (History)		
Muqaddimat Ibn Khaldoun	Abdul Rehman Ibn Khuldun	1406
Taareekh akh-khalifaa	Jalaaluddeen Siyuti	1505
Taareekh Abi Al-fidaa	Jalaluldeen Siyuti	1345
Daroos at-Taareekh al-Islaamee	Muhiuddeen Khiyaat	1345

Source: Derived and translated from *Deeni Madaris ka Nizam-e-Taleem [The Educational System of Religious School].* Islamabad: Institute for Policy Studies, 1987.

Notes

Glossary

1. Mumtaz Ahmad, "Madrassah Education in Pakistan and Bangladesh," in *Religious and Radicalism and Security in South Asia*, ed. Satu Limaye, Robert Wirsing, and Mohan Malik (Honolulu: Asia-Pacific Center for Security Studies, 2004), 101–15; Francis Robinson, *The Ulema of Farangi Mahall and Islamic Culture in South Asia* (Lahore: Feroze Sons, 2002); Tariq Rahman, "Madrassahs: The Potential for Violence in Pakistan?" 2005. http://www.tariqrahman.com/edumain.htm (accessed March 9, 2007).

Introduction

1. See, among others, Jessica Stern, "Pakistan's Jihad Culture," *Foreign Affairs* 79, no. 6 (2000): 115–26, and Stern, "Meeting with the Muj," *Bulletin of the Atomic Scientists* 57, no. 1 (January-February 2001): 42–50; Peter Singer, "Pakistan's Madrassahs: Ensuring a System of Education not Jihad," Brookings Institution Analysis Paper 41 (Washington, D.C.: Brookings Institution, 2001); Robert Looney, "A U.S. Strategy for Achieving Stability in Pakistan: Expanding Educational Opportunities," *Strategic Insights* 7, no. 7 (2002); International Crisis Group, *Pakistan: Madrassahs, Extremism, and the Military*, ICG Asia Report 36 (Islamabad, 2002); Christopher Candland, "Religious Education and Violence in Pakistan," in *Pakistan 2005*, ed. Charles H. Kennedy and Cynthia Botterton (Oxford: Oxford University Press 2006), 230–255; Alexander Evans, "Understanding Madrasahs," *Foreign Affairs* 85, no. 1 (January–February 2006), 9–16; Mathew J. Nelson, "Muslims, Markets, and the Meaning of a 'Good' Education in Pakistan," *Asian Survey* 46, no. 5 (2006) 690–720; Peter Bergen and Swati Pandey, "The Madrassah Scapegoat," *Washington Quarterly* 29, no. 2 (Spring 2006): 117–25; Husain Haqqani, "Madrassas: Knowledge or the 'Shade of Swords,'" *Daily Star* (Beirut) April 21, 2004.

2. I conducted elements of this research in collaboration with the National Bureau of Asian Research (NBAR). In support of the NBAR effort, I developed a questionnaire for different kinds of interview participants. Questions were based on standard guidance provided by the NBAR research managers. These interviews were conducted in February 2006.

3. The Institute for Conflict Management, "Sectarian Violence in Pakistan," updated February 13, 2007, http://www.satp.org/satporgtp/countries/pakistan/database/sect-killing.htm (accessed March 9, 2007).

4. Amir Wasim, "Terrorism Dogs Pakistan in '06: Over 900 Killed in 657 Attacks," *Dawn* (Karachi), January 7, 2007.

5. Stern, "Pakistan's Jihad Culture," and Stern, "Meeting with the Muj."

6. Singer, "Pakistan's Madrassahs"; Looney, "A U.S. Strategy for Achieving Stability in Pakistan."

7. International Crisis Group, *Pakistan*.

8. Richard G. Lugar, Senate Committee on Foreign Relations, Opening Statement for Hearing on Combating Terrorism through Education: The Near East and South Asian Experience, April 19, 2005, http://www.senate.gov/~foreign/testimony/2005/LugarStatement050419.pdf(accessed March 9, 2007).

9. William Dalrymple, "Inside the Madrasas," *New York Review of Books*, 52, no. 19, December 1, 2005, http://www.nybooks.com/articles/article-preview?article_id=18514.

10. This figure of 1 percent is drawn from Tahir Andrabi, Jishnu Das, Asim Ijaz Khwaja, and Tristan Zajonc, "Religious School Enrollment in Pakistan—A Look at the Data" (Washington, D.C.: World Bank, February 8, 2005), http://papers.ssrn.com/sol3/papers.cfm?abstract_id=667843 (accessed March 9, 2007). The limitations of this study are discussed later in this report.

11. Bergen and Pandey, "The Madrassah Scapegoat."

12. Marc Sageman, *Understanding Terrorist Networks* (Philadelphia: University of Pennsylvania Press, 2004).

13. Evans, "Understanding Madrasahs."

14. For a comprehensive inventory of popular press reports, see Andrabi et al., "Religious School Enrollment in Pakistan."

15. Mumtaz Ahmad, "Continuity and Change in the Traditional System of Islamic Education: The Case of Pakistan," in *Pakistan 2000*, ed. Craig Baxter and Charles H. Kennedy (Karachi: Oxford University Press, 2001); Jamal Malik, *Colonialization of Islam: Dissolution of Traditional Institutions in Pakistan* (Columbia, Mo.: South Asia Books, 1998); M.Q. Zaman, "Religious Education and the Rhetoric of Reform: The Madrassah in British India and Pakistan," *Comparative Studies in Society and History* 41, no. 2, 294–323; J.D. Kraan, *Religious Education in Islam with Special Reference to Pakistan: An Introduction and Bibliography* (Rawalpindi: Christian Study Center, 1984); Barbara D. Metcalf, *Islamic Revival in British India: Deoband 1860-1900* (Princeton, N.J.: Princeton University Press, 1982); Robinson, *The Ulema of Farangi Mahall and Islamic Culture in South Asia*.

16. The IPS is considered to be a Jamaat-i-Islami think tank. Its chair and founder, Khurshid Ahmed, is also a vice ameer (vice president) of the Jamaat-Islami (JI), as well as a serving JI senator. IPS does not advertise these connections on its Web site and is opaque about its funding sources. Pakistani analysts believe that IPS is funded through JI charities. See http://www.ips.org.pk/ (accessed March 9, 2007) and http://www.jamaat.org/leadership (accessed March 9, 2007). Probably because of these connections to an important religiopolitical party, IPS has executed several fine studies of Pakistan's madaris. See, for example, *Deeni Madaris ka Nizam-e-Taleem [The Educational System of Religious School]* (Islamabad:IPS, 1987); Saleem Mansoor Khalid, ed., *Deeni Madaaris main taaleem* [Education in Religious Schools] (Islamabad: IPS, 2002); and *Pakistan Religious Education Institutions, an Overview—An IPS Taskforce Report* (Islamabad: IPS, 2002). Also see Tariq Rahman, *Denizens of Alien Worlds: A Study of Education Inequality and Polarization in Pakistan* (Karachi: Oxford University Press, 2004); Rahman, "Pluralism and Intolerance in Pakistani Society Attitudes of Pakistani Students Towards the Religious 'Other,'" last revised

October 30, 2003 (paper presented at a conference on pluralism at Aga Khan University, Institute for the Study of Muslim Civilization, October 25, 2003). For government figures, see Government of Pakistan, *Deeni Madaris ki Jame Report [Complete Report of Religious Schools]* Islamic Education Research Cell (Islamabad: Ministry of Education, 1988). An earlier document was *Report: Qaumi Komiti Barai Deeni Madaris [Report of the Committee for Religious School]* (Islamabad: Ministry of Religious Affairs, 1979). Khalid also cites a report by the Ministry of Education published in 2000. However, he provides no information about this report. See, for example, his note to chart 10, 168.

17. Saleem Ali, "Islamic Education and Conflict: Understanding the Madrassahs of Pakistan," unpublished working draft, August 2005, http://www.uvm.edu/~envprog/madrassah/Ali-Madrassah-draft-8-15-05.pdf.

18. Ideally, to explore the links between madrassah density and violence, one would need to select four kinds of areas: 1) low violence, low madrassah penetration; 2) low violence, high madrassah penetration; 3) high violence, low madrassah penetration; and 4) high violence, high madrassah penetration. However, collecting these data would be prohibitively costly. For this reason, Ali relied on convenience sampling.

19. Tahir Andrabi et al., "Religious Education"; Social Policy and Development Center, *Social Development in Pakistan Annual Review 2002–03—The State of Education*, http://www.spdc-pak.com/publications/sdip2003.asp.

20. Andrabi et al., "Religious Education."

21. The excluded areas vary by survey instrument (census or Pakistani Integrated Household Survey) and by year. In 1991, for example, the PIHS sample frame completely excluded the Federally Administered Tribal Areas, Kashmir, military restricted areas, and the districts of Kohistan, Chitral, Malakand, and protected areas of the NWFP. It also excluded households that depended entirely on charity for their sustenance. For the 1991 wave, Pakistan's Federal Bureau of Labor Statistics estimated that about 4 percent of Pakistan's population was excluded from the sampling frame. World Bank, "Basic Information: Pakistani Integrated Household Survey" (1991), Poverty and Resources Division, December 1995, http://www.worldbank.com/lsms/country/pk91/pk91.pdf (accessed February 11, 2007). In contrast, in the 2001 wave, the PIHS sample universe consisted of all urban and rural areas of all four provinces, Azad Jammu and Kashmir, FATA, and Northern Areas as defined by the provincial governments. It excluded military restricted areas and protected areas of NWFP. In total the sample frame excluded about 2 percent of Pakistan's population. As a result, data on educational choices are not available in these sensitive areas. See Pakistan Federal Bureau of Statistics, "Sample Design of Pakistan Integrated Household Survey (PIHS) 2001–02," March 2005, http://www.statpak.gov.pk/depts/fbs/statistics/pihs2000-2001/pihs2001-02_6.pdf (accessed February 11, 2007). See also Pakistan Federal Bureau of Statistics, "Pakistan Integrated Household Survey (PIHS) Round IV: 2001–2002: Basic Education," http://www.statpak.gov.pk/depts/fbs/statistics/pihs2000-2001/pihs2000-2001.html (accessed February 12, 2007). Also, the Pakistan Census of 1998 fielded only a limited survey instrument in FATA, which tended to collect only basic informationout household

size, age, literacy, educational attainment, and physical infrastructure of localities. For more information about the census, see Pakistan's Population Census Organization's Website, http://www.statpak.gov.pk/depts/pco/statistics/statistics.html#Pop (accessed March 9, 2007)

22. I had several methodological conversations with the team leader in March 2007. Because the census fielded only an abbreviated form of the census instrument in FATA in 1998, and because PIHS has too few households from FATA in the sample, they were unable to use standard imputation techniques to estimate prevalence of full-time madrassah utilization in FATA

23. Under the auspices of the United Nations of Assistance Mission to Afghanistan (UNAMA), the author conducted extensive fieldwork in Afghanistan and Pakistan to investigate the recruitment of suicide attackers between June and September 2007. Data gathered from interviews with UNAMA field researchers, Afghan police and intelligence officials, international military and diplomatic staff, as well as journalist and analysts within Pakistan consistently suggest that madaris in North Waziristan and South Waziristan provide suicide attackers for both the Afghan and Pakistani theaters.

24. For an extensive review of the problem of the 1998 census, see Anita M. Weiss, "Much Ado about Counting: The Conflict over Holding a Census in Pakistan," *Asian Survey* 39, no. 4 (July-August 1999): 679–93.

25. Ibid.

26. Ibid.

27. Former Minister for Religious Affairs Mahmood Ahmed Ghazi estimated that as many as 1.7 million children attend madaris. Although he did not specify whether this figure included full-time and part-time enrollments, it represents about 8 percent of school-going children (19.92 million). Ghazi mentioned this figure during an interview with the International Crisis Group in April 2002. See International Crisis Group, *Pakistan.*

28. Tahir Andrabi, Jishnu Das, and Asim Ijaz Khwaja, "Private Schooling: Limits and Possibilities," World Bank Working Paper, October 2005; and Social Policy and Development Center, Social Development in Pakistan Annual Review 2002–03—The State of Education.

29. For a discussion of this survey, its results and analytical framework, see C. Christine Fair, "Militant Recruitment in Pakistan: A New Look at the Militancy-Madrassah Connection," *Asia Policy*, 1, no. 4 (July 2007): 107–134. Also see Victor Asal, C. Christine Fair, and Stephen Shellman, "Consenting to Jihad: Insights from A Survey of 140 Militant Families in Pakistan," February 28, 2007 (paper presented at the International Studies Association forty-eighth annual meeting), accessible (by ISA members)at the ISA Conference Archive, http://archive.allacademic.com/one/isa/isa07/index.php?cmd=isa07.

30. Ethan Bueno de Mesquita, "The Quality of Terror," *American Journal of Political Science* 49, no. 3 (July 2005): 515–30; Bergen, "The Madrassah Scapegoat"; Evans, "Understanding Madrasahs"; Alan B. Krueger and Jitka Maleckova, "The Economics and the Education of Suicide Bombers," *New Republic* 24 (June 2002):

27–34; Claude Berrebi, "Evidence about the Link Between Education, Poverty and Terrorism among Palestinians," Princeton University Industrial Relations Working Paper 477 (2003); Sageman, *Understanding Terrorist Networks*; Alan B. Krueger and Jitka Maleckova. "Education, Poverty, Political Violence, and Terrorism: Is There a Causal Connection?" National Bureau of Economic Research Working Paper 9074 (2002).

31. Author fieldwork for UNAMA in Afghanistan and Pakistan between June and September 2006. The author met with a variety of Afghan police and intelligence officials, as well as international military and diplomatic analysts, in Afghanistan. Meetings were also held in Pakistan in July with numerous analysts and journalists who follow this subject.

32. Rahman, "Madrassahs."

33. The Lal Masjid was a known militant mosque with strong connections to Deobandi sectarian groups and groups operating in Kashmir. Observers in Pakistan have remarked to me that this is an important case in which Pakistan has encountered difficulties in continuing to manage its erstwhile proxies.

34. This view was repeatedly expressed during my February 2006 fieldwork. However, as one anonymous reviewer of this report noted, Islamist political parties are calling for more Islamic studies in nonreligious fields. This view was also expressed by a madrassah administrator, Qazi Abdul Qadeer Khamosh, who spoke at the United States Institute of Peace on February 5, 2007. This event featured madrassah administrators who have participated in the madrassah training program operated by the International Center for Religion and Diplomacy in Washington, D.C. A recording of his comments is at "Promoting Peace and Tolerance through Madrasa Reform," February 5, 2007, United States Institute of Peace, http://www.usip.org/events/2007/0205_madrasa_reform.html.

1. Contextualizing Islamic Education in Pakistan

1. Pakistanis prefer the terms "mainstream" and "worldly" to the word "secular" because the Urdu translation of secular is usually "bemazhab" or "ladeeniyat," which literally means "without religion."

2. For more information about Pakistan's school system, see Tariq Rahman, "Education in Pakistan: a Survey," in *Pakistan on the Brink: Politics, Economics, and Society*, ed. Craig Baxter (Karachi: Oxford University Press, 2004), 171–190.

3. Rukhsana Zia, "Religion and Education in Pakistan: An Overview," *Prospects* 33, no. 2 (June 2003): 165–78.

4. Note that Punjabi is not the language of instruction in Punjab; Urdu is.

5. For differing discussions of this topic see Rahman, "Education in Pakistan," and World Education Service (Canada), "World Education Profiles: Pakistan-Education Overview," May 6, 2004, http://www.wes.org/ca/wedb/pakistan/pakdov.htm (accessed March 9, 2007).

6. In addition to mainstream and religious education, the Provincial Education and Labor Departments administer several vocational and technical education pro-

grams. For male vocational institutions, applicants must have completed the eighth grade. These programs generally last two to three years. In contrast, female vocational education programs require a minimum attainment standard of the fifth grade. See World Education Service (Canada), "World Education Profiles: Pakistan—Education Overview."

7. The curricula for classes one to ten may be accessed on the Pakistan Ministry of Education Web site (http://www.moe.gov.pk/).

8. Government of Pakistan, "The New Education Policy of the Government of Pakistan," (1970): 15, quoted in Rukhsana Zia, "Religion and Education in Pakistan," 167.

9. A.H. Nayyar, *The Subtle Subversion: The State of Curricula and Textbooks in Pakistan* (Islamabad: Sustainable Policy Development Institute, 2003).

10. World Education Service (Canada), "World Education Profiles."

11. There is one exception: The Federal Bureau of Statistics published *Census of Private Educational Institutions in Pakistan, 1999–2000*. However, I was not able to obtain this report despite requesting it.

12. This effort is called the National Educational Management Information System (NEMIS), and it will be responsible for collecting education data at the district level in each province and providing them to the education ministry. For more information, see the Web site of the ministry's Academy of Educational Planning and Management, http://www.aepam.gov.pk/Nemis.htm (accessed March 9, 2007).

13. Andrabi et al., "A Dime a Day."

14. Tahir Andrabi, Jishnu Das, and Asim Ijaz Khwaja, "Private Schooling: Limits and Possibilities"; Tahir Andrabi, Jishnu Das, and Asim Ijaz Khwaja, "The Rise of Private Schooling in Pakistan: Catering to the Urban Elite or Educating the Rural Poor?" Unpublished working paper, March 21, 2002. http://www.economics. pomona.edu/Andrabi/Research/Pakschool%20March29.pdf. (accessed March 9, 2007).

15. See Harold Alderman, Peter F. Orazen, and Elizabeth M. Paterno, "School Quality, School Cost, and the Pubic/Private School Choices of Low-Income Households in Pakistan," *Journal of Human Resources* 36 (Spring 2001): 304–26.

16. I visited a branch in Lahore in February 2006. It charges an admission fee of Rs.3500 ($58.51), an annual fee of Rs.500 ($8.35), another fee of Rs.500 ($8.35) for computers and other facilities, and a monthly fee of Rs.600 ($10.02). A percentage of students cannot afford these fees, so the school does provide concessions to them if they apply for financial aid. School administrators explained that between 23 and 34 percent of their students have received such concessions.

17. Mathew J. Nelson, "Muslims, Markets."

18. Interview with principal of boys' section of Iqra Rauzatul Aftfal Trust, Shakh (branch) Sayyadina Said Bin Zaid, Chuni Amar Suddoo (Ferozepur Road), Lahore, February 2006.

19. Ibid.

20. Ibid.

21. During interviews I expressed some surprise at this expectation. The principal explained that memorization of the Quran is so rigorous that it trains young people to acquire knowledge more easily than students who have not memorized the Quran. My visits to classrooms provided no insights into whether or not students mastered such material in one year.

22. In Pakistan, each province has several boards of intermediate and secondary education (BISE) that prescribe courses of instruction, ensure provision of requisite facilities for affiliated institutions, conduct exams, and appoint examiners and supervisory staff. In addition to the four provinces of Punjab, Sindh, Baluichistan, and Northwest Frontier Province, there is also the Federal Board of Intermediate and Secondary Education (FBISE) Islamabad, which has jurisdiction over affiliated schools in the Islamabad Capital Territory, throughout Pakistan's cantonments and garrisons, Federally Administered Northern Areas, and Pakistani schools abroad. There is also the Armed Forces Board for Higher Edcuation located within the Army Education Directorate at army headquareters in Rawalpindi.

23. Interview with the principal of the boys' section of the Iqra Rauzatul Aftfal Trust, Shakh (branch) Sayyadina Said Bin Zaid, Chuni Amar Suddoo (Ferozepur Road), Lahore, February 2006.

24. See the Web site of the Arqam Academy, http://www.muslims.ws/arqum/intro.html.

25. For detailed information about subjects and textbooks used at each level, see Arqan Academy's course listing, http://www.muslims.ws/arqum/course.htm.

26. See Al Huda International's Web site at http://www.alhudapk.com/ (accessed March 9, 2007).

27. I visited a Jamaat-i-Islami private school and clinic in Mardan. They were located across the alleyway from the madrassah I visited in February 2006.

28. See Christopher Candland, "Religious Education and Violence in Pakistan," 239.

29. Ibid.

30. Interview with teachers and administrators at Jamia Tafeem ul Quran, a Jamaat-i-Islam madrassah in Mardan, February 2006.

31. Interview with principal and vice-principal of Darul Uloom Islamiya (Barakoh Rd., Islamabad), February 2006.

32. Fieldwork in February 2006. These schools have been established by some of the most prestigious madaris in Pakistan, such as Kher-ul-Madaris (Multan) and Jamia Ashrafiya (Lahore). Jamaat-i-Islami madaris also have been active in establishing "public schools" for students. These schools are so new that they have yet to produce a cohort.

33. Interviews in Pakistan, February 2006.

34. Interviews in Pakistan with government officials, think-tank analysts, religious scholars, and madrassah officials, February 2006.

35. Dietrich Reetz, "Islamic Education and Worldly Knowledge—The New Gen-

eration of Muslim Schools" (paper presented at the nineteenth European Conference on Modern South Asian Studies, Leiden, June 27–30, 2006).

36. Each of the three armed services has established foundations for its beneficiaries (retired military personnel). For a discussion of the army's foundation (Fauji Foundation), see Col (Ret.) Eas Bokhari, "Fauji Foundation—Profile of a Welfare Organisation for Ex-Servicemen," *Defence Journal* (January 1999), http://www.defencejournal.com/jan99/fauji.htm.

37. Tariq Rahman, "Passports to Privilege," *Peace and Democracy in South Asia* 1, no. 1 (January 2005): 28.

38. Ibid.

39. Ibid, 24–44.

40. Ibid, 27.

41. For example, see http://www.darsequran.com, which offers materials online to study the Quran and Hadiths, as well as links to acquire documents published in print and on CD. Other Web sites, such as http://www.tanzeem.org/, help people find Quran study circles near them and facilitate the study of the Quran. In fact, there has been a fast proliferation of online library resources for Dars-i-Quran, such as http://tauheed-sunnat.com/a/downloads-cat311.html; http://www.tanzeem.org.pk/broadcast/audio/urdu/mnunew01.htm;http://www.tazkeer.org/audio/dars.php, and others.

42. Social Policy and Development Centre, *Social Development in Pakistan, 2002–03* (Islamabad, 2003): 171–173.

43. Government of Pakistan, *Education for All: The Year 2000—Assessment Pakistan Country Report* (Islamabad: Ministry of Education, October 1999), http://www2.unesco.org/wef/countryreports/pakistan/rapport_1.html; Faryal Khan, "Case Study on Special Needs Education in Pakistan: The Process of Inclusion," *European Journal of Special Needs Education* 13, no. 1 (1998): 98–111.

44. Khalid Rahman and Syed Rashad Bukhari, "Pakistan: Religious Education Institutions," *Muslim World* 96 (April 2006): 325.

45. Interview with Maulana Taqi Usmani, head of Banuri Town madrassah, February 27, 2006, in Karachi.

46. For various discussions about the differences between madaris and makatib, see Ahmad, "Madrassa Education in Pakistan and Bangladesh," 101–15.

47. Rahman, Khalid, "Pakistan: Religious Education Institutions," 325–26.

48. Zia, "Religion and Education in Pakistan," 169.

49. Ibid, 169–170.

50. Ibid, 169–170.

51. Ibid, 170–172.

52. Social Policy and Development Center, *Social Development in Pakistan*. These data are also available for 1975, 1980, 1990, and 1995 for each of Pakistan's four provinces. Also see United Nations Development Index data for Pakistan, http://

hdr.undp.org/statistics/data/countries.cfm?c=PAK(accessed March 9, 2007).

53. Population Council, *Adolescents and Youth in Pakistan 2001–2002: A Nationally Representative Survey* (New York, Islamabad, 2003): 45, 50, http://www.popcouncil. org/mediacenter/newsreleases/AYSP.html (accessed March 9, 2007).

54. For more information about probabilities of school enrollment and retention rates, see Yasayuki Sawada and Michael Lokshin, "Household Decisions in Rural Pakistan," World Bank Development Research Group, Poverty and Human Resources, Policy Research Working Paper 2541 (February 2001). Their findings generally concurred with those of an earlier 1999 study by Jessica Holmes, "Measuring the Determinants of School Completion in Pakistan: Analysis of Censoring and Selection Bias," Center Discussion Paper 794 (New Haven, Conn.: Yale University, January 1999).

55. For information on madrassah enrollments across time, see Andrabi, "Religious School Enrollment in Pakistan—A Look at the Data."

56. PIHS 2001, compiled and published by Social Policy and Development Center, *Social Development in Pakistan Annual Review,* and Federal Bureau of Statistics, Government of Pakistan, "Household Integrated Economic Survey Round 4: 2001-02 Summary Report" (Islamabad, April 2003), http://www.statpak.gov.pk/ depts/fbs/statistics/hies0102/hies0102.html (accessed March 9, 2007).

57. The Andrabi report has been criticized because it adds data collected from numerous villages in the Punjab to household data. Critics, including reviewers of this manuscript, erroneously assert that these data are not valid on the incorrect grounds that in Punjab, madaris may be underutilized compared to other areas, such as the NWFP. These critics fail to realize that the Punjab has the most madaris (and also the most public schools), reflecting the fact that the Punjab is Pakistan's most populated state and has the country's highest population density. Thus Punjab data are imminently valid for this inquiry.

58. Khalid, *Deeni Madaaris main taaleem,* 145.

59. Andrabi, "Religious School Enrollment in Pakistan."

60. Ibid.

61. Ibid.

62. Ibid.

63. In a personal communication (April 25, 2006), Dr. Andrabi noted that although a census was conducted in FATA in 1998, it was done after extensive political negotiations and compromise. The 1998 census had two forms (long and short). The long form was not distributed to all households, but the short form was. The long form collected more detailed information. The short form omitted questions about literacy, migrancy status, schooling, and other matters. Apparently the long form was not used for households in FATA. For this reason, Andrabi et al. could not explore comparable issues in FATA.

64. Sawada and Lokshin, "Household Decisions in Rural Pakistan," and Chaudhary, N.P., and A. Chaudhary, "Incentives for Rural Female Students in Pakistan," BRIDGES Project, Harvard Institute of International Development and the Acad-

emy of Educational Planning and Management, Pakistan Ministry of Education mimeo (Islamabad), quoted in Sawada and Lokshin, "Household Decisions in Rural Pakistan," 17.

65. Sawada and Lokshin, "HouseholdDecisions in Rural Pakistan."

66. Ibid.

67. Nelson, "Muslims, Markets," and Andrabi, "Religious School Enrollment in Pakistan."

68. In his survey of Pakistani citizens in Rawalpindi on local educational demand, Nelson found that parents from all but the most elite socioeconomic strata value religious as opposed to secular education. Moreover, when they were asked about their primary education goal, religious education (defined as an education that creates "good Muslims") garnered the largest share (41 of 104).

69. I participated in a series of discussions with a sitting member of Pakistan's national assembly, who explained that these decreases in defense expenditures have resulted from changes in the ways military budgetary outlays are categorized, rather than a significant decline in military spending. Military retirement benefits (among other indirect military expenditures) were shifted to the civilian budget to produce a decline in defense spending in the 1990s. This was done mostly to appease international creditors. Thus he contended that in real terms (taking both sources of budgetary allocation into account), military expenditures had not declined. (Conversation, November 2004.)

70. These countries include Indonesia, Equatorial Guinea, Cambodia, Pakistan, Guinea, the United Arab Emirates, and Ecuador. See United Nation Development Program, *Human Development Report 2005* (New York: UNDP, 2005), table 11, "Commitment to Education—Public Spending," 256–67.

71. For a historical assessment, see International Crisis Group, *Pakistan: Reforming the Education Sector* (Islamabad/Brussels, October 2004). See also "Education Policy and Reform," in Nayyar and Salim, *Subtle Subversion*, 2–7, and Zia, "Religion and Education in Pakistan," 165–78.

72. This is an adaptation of Embassy of Pakistan, "Education Sector Reforms (ESR) (A Prospective Assessment)," http://www.embassyofpakistan.org/pb6.php (accessed March 9, 2007).

73. See K.Alan Kronstadt, "Education Reform in Pakistan," CRS Report for Congress, Order Code RS22009, December 23, 2004; Embassy of Pakistan, Washington, D.C., "Madarassah [sic] Refrom [sic] in Pakistan," http://www.embassyofpakistan.org/pb5.php (accessed March 9, 2007). See also Candland, "Religious Education and Violence in Pakistan."

74. Ministry of ReligiousAffairs and Zakat and Ushr, http://www.pakistan.gov.pk/divisions/ContentInfo.jsp?DivID=31&cPath=380_386_416_417&ContentID=1436 (accessed March 9, 2007).

75. To address Pakistani perceptions of various educational streams, I use several years of interview data. Most recently I interviewed madrassah administrators, policy analysts, and officials in the education and religious affairs ministries and the

Council of Islamic Ideology in February 2006. These interviews reinforced data on public opinion about Islam, political Islam, and Islamist parties collected during numerous trips to Pakistan since 2002. I also rely heavily on published analyses of several data sets that illuminate Pakistani public opinion about Islam, political Islam, madrassah reform, religious leaders, and other subjects. I also consulted available secondary literature on these issues. These data are from the Pew Foundation, *Herald* (Karachi, Pakistan), Zogby, Gallup, and the U.S. State Department.

76. In 1834 Thomas B. Macaulay took a position at the Supreme Council of India, where he played a primary role in promoting education in India; he is widely credited with creating the current framework of Pakistan's system of public education. See Thomas B. Macaulay, "Minute of 2 February 1835 on Indian Education," *Macaulay, Prose and Poetry*, selected by G.M. Young (Cambridge: Harvard University Press, 1957), 721–24, 729.

77. See Andrabi, "Religious School Enrollment in Pakistan," 17.

78. Nelson, "Muslims, Markets."

79. Ibid.

80. This is considered to be a model madrassah, and it charges no fees.

81. These data were obtained by the U.S. State Department in 2002 and used with permission. See figure 16 in C. Christine Fair and Karthik Vaidyanathan, "The Practice of Islam In Pakistan and the Influence of Islam on Pakistani Politics," in *Prospects for Peace in South Asia*, ed. Rafiq Dossani and Henry S. Rowen (Stanford, Calif.: Stanford University Press, 2005), 75–108.

82. Ibid.

83. The Pew Global Attitudes Project, www.pewglobal.org (accessed March 9, 2007).

84. Ibid.

2. A Deeper Look at Pakistan's Islamic Schools

1. Al Huda is a chain of schools established by Dr. Farhat Naseem Hashmi to impart religious instruction to women and girls. Al Huda is Jamaat-i-Islami in orientation, and Hashmi herself is in the Jamaat-i-Islami's women's wing. She began Al Huda in Islamabad, and it has spread throughout Pakistan. Hashmi has a Salafi-Wahhabi background; her firebrand oratory draws as many as 5,000 women who come to hear her at any given time. Her message is also spread through audiocassettes and CDs. Despite an outlook that many interviewees called "right-wing," the organization has attracted elite support and is rapidly gaining popularity in Pakistan's middle class as well. Moreover, Hashmi is a popular speaker in the United States, Canada, the United Kingdom, and elsewhere. (Interviews with Salim Mansoor Khalid; Dr. Khaled Massoud, chairman of the Council for Islamic Ideology; and Ilyas Khan, chief research officer, Council for Islamic Ideology.) For detailed information about locations of Al Huda, courses taught, and certificates offered, see Al Huda International's Web site, http://www.alhudapk.com/ (accessed March 9, 2007).

The Tameer-e-Millat Foundation (TMF) was established as a nonprofit organization in 1987 by a group of expatriate Pakistanis living in the United States. According to TMF's Web site, it operates as a "religious multischool NGO" with 324 primary schools, fifty secondary schools, and fifty adult literacy centers throughout Pakistan. TMF schools are thought to "deliver good education" while also concerning themselves with the "moral development of the students." One of Tameer-i-Millat's objectives is to "promote character building and personality development in students in the light of the teachings of the Holy Quran and Sunnah." Although some analysts note that TMF schools challenge liberal thinking, Tameer-i-Millat schools have been supported enthusiastically by the communities where they are situated. See Web site of Tameer-i-Millat Foundation, http://www.educatepakistan.com/Aims.asp (accessed March 9, 2007). See also Abbas Rashid, ed., *Engaging with Basic Education in Pakistan, SAHE Education Watch Report 2000* (Islamabad: Society for the Advancement of Education, 2000), http://web.mit.edu/bilal/www/education/sahereport2000.pdf (accessed March 9, 2007); Haris Gazdar, *Universal Basic Education in Pakistan: A Commentary on Strategy and Results of a Survey* (Islamabad: SDPI, 1998).

2. See Stern, "Pakistan's Jihad Culture"; Stern, "Meeting with the Muj"; Singer, "Pakistan's Madrassahs"; and Looney, "A U.S. Strategy for Achieving Stability in Pakistan." Also see the comprehensive listing of popular accounts of madaris numbers published in Andrabi et al., "Religious School Enrollment in Pakistan," table A1.

3. Interview with Touquir Shah in Islamabad, February 2006.

4. Government of Pakistan, *Education for All*, http://www2.unesco.org/wef/countryreports/pakistan/rapport_1.html; Faryal Khan, "Case Study on Special Needs Education in Pakistan."

5. Ahmad, "Madrassah Education in Pakistan and Bangladesh"; Robinson, *The Ulema of Farangi Mahall*; Rahman, "Madrassahs: The Potential for Violence in Pakistan?"

6. Ahmad, "Madrassah Education in Pakistan and Bangladesh," 102.

7. Candland, "Religious Education and Violence in Pakistan."

8. Madrassah administrators at Jamia Binnoria, interviewed by the author in February 2006, explained the necessity for a shortened girls' curriculum. If girls were to take the eight-year course, their marriages would be delayed beyond an age generally acceptable to their parents. Thus the abbreviated curriculum accommodates the families' desire for girls to obtain a Dars-i-Nizami education, as well as their requirement for an appropriately timed marriage.

9. During the Mughal period the madaris produced jurists, lawyers, and other state functionaries for the court. Under various treaties bringing parts of the declining Mughal Empire under the control of the East India Company, the company promised to continue using Islamic institutions such as courts in governance. During this period madaris were important sites producing functionaries for these posts. This practice continued until the 1857 mutiny, when the British government formally took control of the subcontinent.

10. According to analysis of the frequency distribution of the century in which the authors lived: About 20 percent lived between the eighth and twelfth centuries; 45 percent lived in the thirteenth through fifteenth centuries; 24 percent lived in the sixteenth through eighteenth centuries; and 20 percent lived in the nineteenth and twentieth centuries. This analysis differs from that of Ahmad, "Madrassah Education in Pakistan and Bangladesh," 102. Ahmad provides no empirical basis for his claims.

11. The continued value ascribed to Seena's volume may result partly from the fact that Muslims revere his early and unprecedented contributions to the world's knowledge of medicine and pathology. Seena's name graces pharmaceutical companies, hospitals, and medical schools throughout the Muslim world. In addition to analysis of texts in appendix B, see Ahmad, "Madrassah Education in Pakistan and Bangladesh," 102. Much of this draws from discussions with madrassah teachers and administrators in Pakistan, February 2006. Madrassah administrators at Jamia Binnoria interviewed in February 2006.

12. International Crisis Group, *Pakistan: The Mullahs and the Military* (Brussels, March 2003).

13. See Naveed Ahmed, "Sanad-holders Cannot Contest Local Body Polls: Supreme Court," *News* (Lahore), August 30 2005; International Crisis Group, *Pakistan's Local Polls: Shoring up Military Rule* (Brussels, November 2005).

14. Some scholars say that there are only three Sunni boards, one Shia and Jamaat-i-Islami (JI). They do so because JI claims to be suprasectarian. This nomenclature follows what JI likes to say about itself, and some of these scholars are adherents of JI. However, since my view is that JI is decidedly a Sunni organization, it is classified as such herein.

15. Rahman, *Denizens of Alien Worlds*.

16. Candland, "Religious Education and Violence in Pakistan"; Nayyar, "Madrassa Education: Frozen in Time," in *Education and the State: Fifty Years of Pakistan*, ed. Pervez Hoodboy (Karachi: Oxford University Press, 1998).

17. See Metcalf, Islamic Revival in British India.

18. The six parties that comprise the MMA (United Council of Action) are the Jamaat-I Islami, Jamiat Ulema-e-Pakistan (Noorani), Jamiat Ulema-e-Islam (Fazlur Rehman), Jamiat Ulema-e-Islam (Sami ul Haq), Islami Tehreek-e-Pakistan, and the Markazi Jamiat Al-Hadith (Sajid Mir group).

19. Zahid Hussain, *Frontline Pakistan: The Struggle with Militant Islam* (New York: Columbia University Press, 2007).

20. See Metcalf, *Islamic Revival in British India*.

21. See Claudia Preckel, "Educational networks and scholarly culture in the Islamic principality of Bhopal: Muhammad Siddiq Hasan Khan (1832–1890) and the beginnings of the Ahl-e hadith-movement," (no date), http://www.ruhr-uni-bochum.de/orient/claudia.htm; Rahman, *Denizens of Alien Worlds*.

22. See Stephen P. Cohen on the JI, *The Idea of Pakistan*, 164–65, as well as Seyyed Vali Reza Nasr, *The Vanguard of the Islamic Revolution: The Jama`at-i-Islami of Paki-*

stan (Berkeley: University of California Press, 1994).

23. Nasr, *Vanguard of the Islamic Revolution.*

24. Nasr, *Vanguard of the Islamic Revolution*; and Rahman, *Denizens of Alien Worlds.*

25. Hussain, *Frontline Pakistan*; Mohammad Amir Rana, *A to Z of Jehadi Organizations in Pakistan* (Lahore: Mashal Books, 2004).

26. Rahman, *Denizens of Alien Worlds.*

27. Binori Town was an exception: It has several Ph.D.-qualified teachers.

28. The overrepresentation of high-quality schools is because the lower-quality madaris, as well as the primary and secondary madaris, denied access to me and my research associate.

3. Madaris and Militancy

1. Christine Fair, "Militant recruitment in Pakistan."

2. Krueger, "The Economics and the Education of Suicide Bombers"; Berrebi, "Evidence about the Link between Education, Poverty and Terrorism among Palestinians"; Sageman, *Understanding Terrorist Networks*; Bergen, "The Madrassah Scapegoat." All of these works suffer from at least one serious shortcoming: They ignore the fact that terrorists impose quality standards. Thus, even if poorer and less-educated persons are more likely to want to become terrorists, groups need not take them, as long as there are fewer available terrorist positions than applicants. Their work explains more about what organizations want in their operatives than about the characteristics of people who want to be terrorists.

3. Krueger, "Education, Poverty, Political Violence and Terrorism"; Krueger, "The Economics and the Education of Suicide Bombers"; Berrebi, "Evidence about the Link between Education, Poverty and Terrorism among Palestinians;" Sageman, *Understanding Terror Networks*, 61–98; Bergen, "The Madrassah Scapegoat." 117–125.

4. Fieldwork between June and September 2007 in Afghanistan and Pakistan with the United Nations Assistance Mission in Afghanistan to document the nature of suicide attackers and their perpetrators in Afghanistan and Pakistan.

5. For more information about this survey and its results, see Fair, "Militant Recruitment in Pakistan," and Victor Asal, C. Christine Fair, and Stephen Shellman, "Consenting to Jihad: Insights from Pakistan" (paper presented at the International Studies Association Meeting, February 28, 2007), www.isanet.org; C. Christine Fair, "Who are Pakistan's Militants and their Families?" *Terrorism and Political Violence* 20, no. 1 (forthcoming, winter 2008).

6. Ibid.

7. Paul Collier, "Rebellion as a Quasi-Criminal Activity," *Journal of Conflict Resolution* 44, no. 6 (December 2000): 838–52; Paul Collier and Anke Hoeffler, "Greed and Grievance in Civil War," World Bank Policy Research Paper 2355 (May 2000).

8. Bueno de Mesquita, "The Quality of Terror," 515–530.

9. Ibid.

10. Fieldwork on suicide attackers for UNAMA in Pakistan and Afghanisan between June and September 2007.

11. See the Rendon Group, "Polling Results-Afghanistan Omnibus May 2007," June 15, 2007; Pew Global Attitudes Project, Global Opinion Trends 2002–2007: A Rising Tide Lifts Mood In The Developing World, July 24, 2007, www.pew-global.org/reports/pdf/257.pdf.

12. Pew Global Attitudes Project, Global Opinion Trends 2002–2007.

13. United Nations Department of Safety and Security Afghanistan, "Topic Assessment 01–07: The Phenomenon of Suicide Attacks in Afghanistan," July 3, 2007.

14. Brian Glyn Williams, "The Taliban Fedayeen: The World's Worst Suicide Bombers," *Terrorism Monitor* 5, no. 14 (July, 2007): 1–3.

15. Fieldwork on suicide attackers for UNAMA in Pakistan and AFghanisan between June and September 2007. Also see Williams, "The Taliban Fedayeen."

16. Higher-aptitude persons may be more likely to turn to terrorism when the economy is weak and jobs are in short supply. When the economy is good, high-quality persons generally have access to more lucrative jobs than their low-quality counterparts, and the cost of leaving a good job to participate in a terrorist movement is relatively high. That helps explain why engineers and other technical persons with a history of underemployment become involved in terrorism. They are both available and desired by terrorist organizations, particularly during periods of economic stagnation and downturn. See Bueno de Mesquita, "The Quality of Terror," and Christine Fair and Husain Haqqani, "Think Again: Sources of Islamist Terrorism," *Foreign Policy Online*, January 30, 2006, www.foreignpolicy.com/story/files/story3359.php.

17. Berrebi attempts to deal with the first kind of self-selection, but others, such as Krueger and Maleckova, do not. Moreover, none of these teams deals with the other selection or screening biases—nor do these researchers discuss these biases or the limitations they impose on their conclusions. This is particularly surprising for labor economists, who routinely adjust for these kinds of selection processes in the course of other inquiries by using several available corrective techniques, such as the Heckman Selection Correction procedure. For a thorough critique, see Christina Paxson, "Comment on Alan Krueger and Jitka Maleckova, 'Education, Poverty, and Terrorism: Is There a Causal Connection?'" (Princeton, N.J.: Princeton University Research Program in Development Studies, May 8, 2002), http://www.wws.princeton.edu/~rpds/downloads/paxson_krueger_comment.pdf. For a more general review of this literature, see Nicholas Sambanis, "Poverty and the Organization of Political Violence: A Review and Some Conjectures," (Washington, D.C.: Brookings Institution, July 12, 2004,http://www.brook.edu/es/commentary/journals/tradeforum/papers/200405_ambanis.pdf.

18. This is distinguished from other uses of the term "demand," which could refer to groups' demand for terrorist labor. For a more thorough discussion of demand-side issues, see Paxson, "Comment on Alan Krueger," and Laurence R. Iannaccone,

"Sacrifice and Stigma: Reducing Free-Riding in Cults, Communes, and Other Collectives," *Journal of Political Economy* 100, no. 2 (April 1992): 271–291. I am cognizant of the debate about defining terrorism as a "good." For instance, some argue that terrorism is a "public good." Although this debate is very important in understanding terrorism and terrorist groups, the distinction is not germane to this work. For more information about this and related analytical issues, see Iannaccone, "Sacrifice and Stigma," and Harrison, "An Economist Looks at Suicide Terrorism."

19. For one recent exception, see C. Christine Fair and Bryan Shepherd, "Research Note: Who Supports Terrorism? Insights from Fourteen Muslim Countries," *Studies in Conflict and Terrorism* 29, no. 2 (January–February 2006).

20. Because formal madrassah education (the Alim course or Dars-i-Nizami curriculum) starts after completion of Mutavasatta, tenth-grade madrassah students are older than their counterparts in Urdu- and English-medium schools.

21. Rahman, "Pluralism and Intolerance in Pakistani Society."

22. In addition to asking them specific questions about their points of view, Rahman collected basic information about the students (age, class, gender) and teachers (gender, educational level, subjects taught). From both faculty and students he obtained parental employment information (rank, title, occupational status, salary, income, etc.) for both parents where applicable. Few students provided this income information, and most indicated that their mothers did not work. Thus this income information was not available for students.

23. To untangle these different sources of causality, Rahman would have had to interview household members.

24. For a discussion of the putative links between madrassah education and sectarian violence including refutation and comparative religions, see Candland, "Religious Education and Violence in Pakistan." For an alternative view that discounts such connections, see Rahman, "Education in Pakistan."

25. C. Christine Fair and Peter Chalk, *Fortifying Pakistan: The Role of U.S. Internal Security Assistance* (Washington, D.C.: United States Institute of Peace, 2006).

26. Ibid.

27. Ali, *Islamic Education and Conflict.*

28. See data provided by the Institute for Conflict Management, "Sectarian Violence in Pakistan" (updated February 13, 2007), http://www.satp.org/satporgtp/countries/pakistan/database/sect-killing.htm (accessed March 9, 2007), and Amir Wasim, "Terrorism Dogs Pakistan in '06."

4. Government Reforms

1. Many interlocutors, observers, and analysts inside and outside Pakistan use the expression "deeni madrassah" to state clearly that they mean religious schools in particular.

2. Interviews with Minister of Education Lt. Gen (Ret.) Javed Ashraf Qazi, February 2006.

3. Mohammad Imran, "Madrassa Reform Board: ITMD Doesn't Want to Deal with Qazi," *Daily Times* (Lahore), July 7, 2005, http://www.dailytimes.com.pk/default.asp?page=story_11-7-2005_pg7_6 (accessed March 9, 2007).

4. Interviews with Vakil Ahmed Khan, Ministry of Religious Affairs, February 2006.

5. Ibid.

6. Judgments derived from Khalid Rahman, "Pakistan: Religious Education and Institutions," 333, and from interview with Touquir Shah, February 2006. Shah is the former assistant commissioner who was responsible for registering madaris before the law changed.

7. Interviews with Vakil Ahmed Khan, Ministry of Religious Affairs, February 2006.

8. Ibid.

9. Ibid.

10. Ibid.

11. Ibid.

12. Ibid.

13. Massoud Ansari, "Madrassahs Unreformed," *Newsline* (Karachi) August 2007, http://www.newsline.com.pk/NewsAug2007/newsbeat2aug2007.htm.

14. Interview with Maulana Khalid Binnori in Peshawar, February 2006.

15. Interview with Maulana Taqi Usmani in Karachi, February 2006.

16. Interview with Qari Muhammad Haneef Jullandari at Jamia Kher ul Madaris (Multan), February 2006.

17. Interview with Maulana Hafez Khalil Ahmad in Quetta, February 2006. Khalil is the general secretary of JUI-F for Baluchistan and 2006 recipient of an International Visitors Program fellowship from the U.S. State Department.

18. Interview with madrassah administrator in Multan, February 2006.

19. Interview with madrassah administrator in Karachi, February 2006.

20. Interview with Touquir Shah.

21. Interview with madrassah administrator in Karachi, February 2006.

22. During meetings with high-level U.S. State Department officials following my trip, they concurred that this is indeed the U.S. intent with respect to Pakistan's educational system.

23. This view was expressed by nearly every madrassah administrator interviewed for this study.

24. See "Hambali Brother Caught in Pakistan," CNN.com, September 22, 2003, http://edition.cnn.com/2003/WORLD/asiapcf/southeast/09/22/hambali.brother/index.html (accessed March 9, 2007).

25. See the Web site of Jamia Binoria SITE, "Foreign Students' Department," http://www.binoria.org/foreign.asp (accessed March 9, 2007).

26. This is consistent with the empirical findings of Ali, "Islamic Education and Conflict: Understanding the Madrassahs of Pakistan."

5. Conclusions and Implications

1. Discussion with high-level State Department official in Washington, D.C., March 2006.

Index

About the Author

C. CHRISTINE FAIR is a senior political scientist with the RAND Corporation. Before joining RAND she worked in Kabul as a political affairs officer with the United States Assistance Mission to Afghanistan. Her research focuses on South Asian political and military affairs.

Much of this volume was written while the author was a senior research associate at the Center for Conflict Analysis and Prevention of the United States Institute of Peace. Before joining the Institute in April 2004 she was an associate political scientist at the RAND Corporation.

Fair has published on a wide array of issues pertaining to the security competition between India and Pakistan, Pakistan's internal security, the causes of terrorism, and U.S. strategic relations with India and Pakistan. Her recent books include *Fortifying Pakistan: The Role of U.S. Internal Security Assistance* (United States Institute of Peace, 2006), *The Counterterror Coalitions: Cooperation with Pakistan and India* (RAND, 2004), and *Urban Battle Fields of South Asia* (RAND, 2004). She has contributed to numerous multiauthor volumes, such as *Securing Tyrants or Fostering Reform: U.S. Internal Security Assistance to Repressive and Transitioning Regimes, ed.* (Jones et al., RAND, 2006), as well as edited volumes, U.S. Institute of Peace Special Reports, and peer-reviewed journals.

Fair is a graduate of the University of Chicago, where she earned a master's degree from the Harris School of Public Policy and a Ph.D. in South Asian languages and civilizations. She has conducted fieldwork in India, Pakistan, Bangladesh, Sri Lanka, and Iran. She is also managing editor of *India Review*.

United States Institute of Peace

The United States Institute of Peace is an independent, nonpartisan, national institution established and funded by Congress. Its goals are to help prevent and resolve violent conflicts, promote post-conflict stability and development, and increase peacebuilding capacity, tools, and intellectual capital worldwide. The Institute does this by empowering others with knowledge, skills, and resources, as well as by directly engaging in peacebuilding efforts around the globe.

Chairman of the Board: J. Robinson West
Vice Chairman: María Otero
President: Richard H. Solomon
Executive Vice President: Patricia Powers Thomson
Vice President: Charles E. Nelson